10.5.77

BLUEPRINT
FOR
INDUSTRIAL
SURVIVAL

BLUEPRINT
FOR
INDUSTRIAL
SURVIVAL

*What Has Gone Wrong
in Industrial Britain
Since the War?*

by

Viscount Watkinson

PC, CH

London
George Allen & Unwin Ltd
Ruskin House   Museum Street

First published in 1976

© George Allen & Unwin Ltd 1976

ISBN 0 04 658219 3

Printed in Great Britain
in 11 point Baskerville type
by The Devonshire Press
Barton Road, Torquay

Contents

Contents

Chapter 1

WHAT WENT WRONG?

DECLINE—THE RECORD

In 1945 the British were the admiration of the world. By 1975 Britain has sunk to one of the bottom places in the league of industrial growth and efficiency and is often despised rather than admired by other countries. So what has gone wrong? To seek to answer this fundamental question is not to play the old British game of self-denigration. It is to make known much more clearly what has to be put right in British industry and society if the country is to survive as a significant industrial power.

The first seeds of failure were sown in the early postwar years. Self-satisfaction at military victory, against what looked like hopeless odds, obscured the grave risk of industrial defeat in the postwar period. The position of Britain's main industrial competitors at that time should have been examined much more carefully than they were. The USA was totally unscathed, with all the advantages of war-inspired gains in technology and manufacturing capacity. West Germany and Japan were filled with a stern creative determination to win back the prosperity and industrial competitiveness that defeat had taken from them, using an industrial base that was to be modernised and reconstructed by the victorious Allies. Britain alone had to make do with a war-damaged and largely obsolescent industry, while its main European and Eastern competitors were given a fresh start. The British believed too easily that the world owed them a living for 'standing alone' against the dictators; the world paid in relatively short-lived admiration, but in little else. So Britain made a bad start, the more disastrous for its failure to recognise its industrial vulnerability in those early postwar years.

Perhaps Britain could have capitalised on its wartime reputation had it joined Europe in the late 1940s and taken the lead that was there for the asking. Yet there was no national will to do this, as was shown by the free vote in the House of Commons against joining the European Coal and Steel Community, the forerunner of the European Economic Community. So the old prewar British model of plant, industrial relations and technological approach was kept. It was not a bad model and one that had served well; yet it was one that would be immensely strained, however well it was refurbished, to meet the new competition that was to come from friend and foe alike. Some British management and trade union practices too, in those critical years of the late 1940s and early 1950s, like some British plants, were as appropriate to the changing world as the famous old Model T Ford was to an era of jetline travel.

Yet, although there may have been much that was wrong and inappropriate in the national scene in 1945, at least it was still a free enterprise society controlled by the disciplines of a well-tried market economy. Today it is a 'mixed' economy and every postwar government has sought to alter the basic ingredients of the 'mix'. The resulting disruption of the working of the market economy and of the practice of free enterprise has worsened Britain's already weak competitive position. To take only one example: What the British transport system required after the destruction and strain of the war years was modernisation and reorganisation. What it got were the endless delays and compromises arising from the continuing political arguments for and against nationalisation. Whatever the merits of the political arguments, they were not relevant to the immediate problem, which was an urgent requirement for the rebuilding of the British rail, road and shipping services.

Yet despite the political arguments and a reluctance to face fundamental change, the nation was moving inexorably towards a new kind of society. This was to be much more business-centred, with business replacing the older squirearchical concept of national life. Business of one kind or another was to provide over three-quarters of the nation's jobs, most of its tax revenue and the patronage of arts and education that in earlier times had been the personal responsibility of the upper echelons of British society. This advance towards a business-centred society was to impose new strains on all its members. It imposed on directors and managers of public and private companies duties which were far wider than those encompassed by their traditional search for growth and profits. It placed on successive governments and their advisers the responsibility for making complex management judgements, at a time when neither the Civil Service nor ministers of the Crown were trained to take such decisions. These were factors from which revolution could have been born. It says much for British tolerance and political maturity that an immense and continuing change in the whole basis of British society has so far been contained within the framework of its democratic parliamentary system. Yet because of this process of democratic compromise, change has so far brought more industrial disadvantages than the advantages hoped for.

By any comparison, Britain is a poorer and less significant industrial nation than it was thirty years ago. It has no automatic right of survival as an industrial power. As this fact becomes more widely realised there will be a chance, perhaps a last chance, for the nation to react decisively to adverse circumstances, as it has so often done in the past. For the reaction to be successful there will have to be a clear appreciation of the contrary odds and of the steps necessary to overcome them. In other words, agreement will be needed (a) on what has gone wrong in the period since the end of the 1939–45 war, in industrial rather than political terms, and (b) on the action necessary to put national affairs in order. These are practical rather than political problems. They place the main burden of implementation on all the managers of the British economy, for in a mixed economy such as Britain's managers must include those in charge of the industrial departments within the Whitehall machine and those in charge of nationalised industry, as well as those in the private sector.

Are there any broad conclusions to be drawn from past mistakes in the management of the British economy, before a more detailed analysis of precise case history is turned to? There are three issues that appear to be inescapable: the problems of size and scale, of social relationships and of administration.

THE PROBLEM OF SIZE AND SCALE

It is a fundamental fact that, whatever the British may wish their country to be, Britain is in fact a relatively small nation bereft first of an empire and then of a commonwealth world trading base. So the country can no longer afford to play a world role even if it could do it well, as it probably still could. Certainly, it can no longer afford to pay more than its fair share of free world defence unless it gets some material advantage in return. Yet Britain cannot stand alone. So the cold logic of replacing a lost Empire trading base with active membership of a European trading group is undeniable. Delay here, from whatever cause, has held up the essential reshaping of British industry to fit Britain's new position in the world.

Of the one-time special relationship with the USA, little if anything remains. It would be impossible to rebuild it; the disparity in scale is now too great. It is this disparity of scale compared with Britain's larger industrial competitors in world markets that needs to be more clearly understood. Being small imposes severe limitations, particularly in the higher technologies. Britain in the postwar years has led so often in industrial invention and then failed, because of sheer lack of means, to do more than produce the prototype model that taught its competitors how to develop it.

Let us take one of the more famous examples: the jet engine. Britain's development of this new form of propulsion put the country in reach, at the end of the 1939–45 war, of a commanding lead in civil air passenger transport. All industry had to do for Britain to dominate the field of jet passenger transport was to produce a reliable airframe. The failure of the original models of the de Havilland Comet fuselage, to withstand the stresses of flight at jet altitude, taught Britain's American competitors many valuable lessons, particularly as the failure was the subject of prolonged public inquiry in Britain. Even so, the lead could have been recovered by the mid 1950s if more than one project at a time could have been tackled. But Britain just could not afford to run more than one horse in any particular race, whereas the Americans could accept a number of failures and still come through with a winner. So, British civil aviation had to make do with the Britannia prop-jet aircraft, which in its turn had to make do with an engine originally designed for use in flying boats. There was no alternative but to take the risk or get out of the business and this, in due course, led to further major troubles.

The British aero industry, and now the British aerospace industry, has survived these and other difficulties to become one of the country's largest and most consistent earners of foreign exchange. This is a tribute to the industry's outstanding capacity for superb management and innovation. Yet the lesson remains of how much more business could have been done in the world if Britain had known how to overcome the problems of manufacturing scale and development that lie behind the disparate size of American and British industry.

So for the future British industries must try to avoid a 'battle of the giants' with competitors many times larger than themselves. More account must be taken of the fact that, while Britain's inventive resources remain equal to that of any other nation, its physical production capacity is that of a relatively small nation. The logic of combination with Europe is again strong. For example, whatever views one may hold about the

Concorde supersonic passenger jet, there can be no doubt that it could only have been achieved on a combined Anglo–French basis and would have been better secured if West German industry could have been an active partner. The case will always be made that Britain would have been better advised to concentrate more, in the postwar years, on less advanced projects (consumer durables, for example), but the lesson of the advantages of a wider industrial base still remains.

More study should be given to being relatively small and good. This must lead to consideration of how present-day Britain can best concentrate its industrial efforts to produce the maximum efficiency and growth relative to its limited manpower and capital resources. Only in this way can the country successfully meet the challenge of the last quarter of this century. To accept some limitation of size does not imply a strategy of regression and retreat. The world is not yet at the stage where the industrialised nations must consciously try to reduce their industrial and technological base. The very reverse is true. Would Britain be worrying as much about oil if it had been more successful in developing atomic power or modernising coal production? Has Britain any moral right to pull back in the industrial race when at least one-third of the world does not enjoy even the basic minimum requirements for material existence, let alone well-being? The need remains for the British people to be more productive and more efficient if the country is to survive.

THE PROBLEM OF SOCIAL RELATIONSHIPS

Here lies the second fundamental failure of Britain's industrialised society since 1945. The British won a war on the basis of a well-led and united nation meeting overwhelming odds with guts and bravery. In the peace 'blood, sweat and tears' were forgotten and there was a failure to be concerned with the problems of personal leadership and participation in an increasingly remote and technological world. So technological progress was not matched with personal involvement and the British people did not achieve a sense of job satisfaction in the postwar world. The earlier relationship between master and man may have been patronising and paternalistic, but at least it involved face-to-face contact. Too often today, businesses, particularly large businesses, operate in a vacuum as far as personal relationships are concerned. Underestimation of the constantly accelerating rate of change has failed to create a capacity to handle the problems of individuals facing such change. Since 1945 Britain has made probably the largest investment in education of any Western nation. Yet against this background of a better educated and thus more questioning society, Britain has endeavoured to maintain its rigidly stratified society. Social stratification permeates all sectors of the nation. The trade unions are as status-conscious as employers; one treasures the mythology of Tolpuddle, while the other too often seeks to maintain the Victorian tradition of the 'two sides' of industry.

Meantime, the exploitation of television's strong visual image by the broadcasting companies and the increasing use of television by the advertisers of consumer goods have created a new motivational structure in British society, which uses envy as its driving force. Any free market economy must be fuelled by some degree of expectation/demand relationship, but to remain in balance this has to be of a type that accepts the fact that increased demand can only be met by increased efficiency and hard work over a reasonable time cycle. The pressures of the glossy life pictured by television advertisers and many entertainment programmes create a form of expectation that tends to translate immediately into a demand for entitlement. This new and pressing demand/entitlement relationship increasingly conditions pay negotiations, political pledges and much else. It has certainly done as much to fuel inflation as raw material costs or monetary policy. If consumption continues to be augmented at the expense of investment and regardless of the necessity to earn entitlement by increased effort and efficiency, a level of inflation will be generated that will destroy British society. Just as Britain's technological progress became unbalanced by a failure to impose the discipline of relative scale, so the stimulus of consumer demand needs the control of a wider understanding on the part of ordinary men and women about the way an industrial economy should be kept in balance. The majority of Britain's population may have been provided with the educational background necessary to understand the argument about how to relate demand to supply and to entitlement, but they have not been provided with the facts of the case against inflation in a form which sways their judgement.

People today are increasingly unwilling to accept control from the top. Thus institutions, whether they be of government or of industry, are finding it difficult to impose decisions from the top level without resorting to an unacceptable degree of coercion. People, as they become better educated and as they are more subject to instant briefing about almost every problem by the media, will only accept decisions that seem to them to be relevant to their own individual circumstances. Persuasion has then to start from the roots of society, not from the top. In a highly industrialised and organised society such as Britain's, this means that there must be a feeling of participation and involvement by all those who are organised, a category outside which few people fall today—except babes in arms and the very old. The earlier concept of industry owned by the shareholders, run by the management and operated by the employees just will not meet this situation. Nor will it be met by the stratified organisations of nationalised industry or government agency. So there is an extremely urgent job to be done in the area of human relationships—a job that is fundamental to Britain's successful survival as a nation of any significance. As far as industry is concerned, at least some thought is now being given to the problem by the more far-sighted. As a result, a number of bodies—including the Confederation of British Industry, the Trades Union Congress, the British

Institute of Management, the Institute of Directors and the Industrial Society—are giving more detailed guidance to their members on how to achieve a wider degree of participation.

Perhaps not surprisingly, the viewpoints differ, the TUC preferring the West German model of participation while the management associations opt for variations on a British theme. Government too will be involved, for the Conservative Companies Bill, lost on the change of government in 1974, has given way to a much more mandatory socialist version of government control in the Industry Act. Further legislative pressure is bound to be applied by one government or another. The best summary so far of what is going to be required by managers, in private and nationalised industry and in government to meet a new situation, appears in 'The Responsibilities of the British Public Company' (1973) and 'Industry and Government' (1974), published by the CBI and approved by the 400 members of its Grand Council. Later chapters will refer again to this initiative, which shows clearly how much achievement has fallen short of need in the area of human relations in the postwar years. Again Britain rightly took pride in being the pioneer of formalised employer/worker relationships: the birthplace of the trade union movement and the instigator of much of the modern framework of social and industrial legislation. This pride concealed a steady growth of mythology about the past and a growing substitution of confrontation for co-operation in the attitudes of employees and employers.

THE PROBLEM OF ADMINISTRATION

One final issue must be raised at this stage. If Britain succeeds in relating the scale of its industrial activities to its place in the world, and if it succeeds in getting its human relationships right, then it will have made good progress. Even so, the national effort will still be impeded by an inability to relate the requirements of modern technology to those of parliamentary government. Government must take its time from Parliament, and Parliament still retains much of the timing of the Gladstonian model in its make-up. The Exchequer, however many budgets may be presented in one year, is still governed by its annual accounting period. All expenditure must be balanced off in each current year. Departments that underspend are in nearly as much trouble as those that exceed their estimates, and the constraining consequence for industry is that government expenditure has constitutionally only one year's validity. Ministers' tenure of office and government's tenure of power do not provide a much greater degree of continuity. Governments have at most only five years of life and few run the full course. Ministers come and go with considerable frequency within the life cycle of a government and three years in one office is an unusually long spell. This was tolerable when government and Parliament were concerned with legislation and little else. A minister's senior civil servants could present him with an ably marshalled set of legislative options and he could choose among them. Today, when a government has direct control of more than 50 per cent of the gross national product and a powerful influence over the remainder, a totally different kind of approach is required to the management of the economy. So far this new approach has not been provided and thus the interface between industry and government remains one of almost total incompatibility. Industry, particularly advanced technology-based industry, must plan in five- to ten-year time cycles and must back its plans with very large sums of its shareholders' money. Government prefers to plan from day to day and finds it difficult, if not impossible, to guarantee continuity of policy beyond the annual exchequer accounting period. In special circumstances it may look further ahead, but even then not beyond the uncertain time span of a single government.

Various devices have been brought forward to try to bridge this gap between industry and government. The National

Economic Development Council is one of the more important
bodies that seek to fulfil this task. The NEDC will be examined
in Chapters 6 and 8. Every industry has a sponsoring government department and links are developed here that provide
some degree of continuity of policy. The National Enterprise
Board of Planning Agreements will also play a part. Industrialists, however, suspect (with some reason) that all these arrangements can well be something of a charade so long as Her
Majesty's Treasury has the last word. The Prime Minister is
still First Lord of the Treasury and no minister, however
powerful he or his department may be, can put proposals to the
Cabinet involving new expenditure unless such proposals are
first cleared with the Treasury. Here then is another major
problem that requires a solution if Britain is to learn from past
mistakes and build better for the future.

WHERE THE MANAGER STANDS

None of the issues that this chapter has discussed are strictly
political, in the sense that they are of no concern to British
management. All managers have to operate in a 'mixed'
economy and they must accept that the mix is an odd brew of
private enterprise, state enterprise and direct government
control. It is not unfair to say that in these turbulent years of
political and economic change since the end of the 1939–45
war the nation has created a system that is neither capitalistic
nor socialistic in the full sense of the terms. Nor is the economy
fully subject to the discipline of the free market or to overall
state control. It is indeed 'mixed'! Managers have to live with
the situation as they find it, but they must often feel that all that
has been achieved in the last thirty years is an accentuation of
the worst features of both types of government.

When Britain was a rich and powerful nation backed by the
developing market power of a great empire, almost any degree
of experimentation could be afforded in political and social
life. Today the country is neither rich nor all-powerful, and

thus very few mistakes can be afforded. It may be wise, therefore, to analyse more carefully where the British have gone wrong
in the past three decades. It is, after all, not the world's fault
but Britain's own that it has slipped so far down the league of
industrial efficiency and social and political well-being. There
are many who willingly blame all this on the failure of free
enterprise and a few who advocate the total destruction of the
present system whatever the constituents of the 'mix'. Yet the
facts show that free enterprise still provides the majority of
jobs in Britain. It is free enterprise that has achieved an 80 per
cent increase in British exports over the last ten years. It is free
enterprise that produces much of the tax revenue that pays
for Britain's social services. Destroy free enterprise and the
basic economic sinews of the nation will be destroyed.

So managers today cannot regard their task as being fulfilled
solely by application to their particular management problems.
Their job comes first and must have overall priority. Beyond it
is a further responsibility: that of ensuring that the frame of
reference in which they have to operate is one that takes account
of the circumstances of today. This managers have to do by
seeking to understand more about (a) the political constituents
of a mixed economy, (b) how modern government works, and
(c) the reasons why Britain has not done as well as it perhaps
has deserved to do in this second half of the twentieth century.
So managers are deeply involved in these issues. But to feel
involved is not necessarily to have full understanding of the
problems. To tell a manager that his concept of scale is false,
that his human and social relations are bad and that his relationship with his governing board is highly defective, would be to
make as damning an indictment as possible. These are charges
that can be brought against the nation, and its managers
cannot avoid some of the blame. If they are to be considered as
a spur to remedial action they must be seen to be fully justified
and documented. They must also be capable of being clearly
understood by all those who will have to play a part in providing the remedy. This understanding requires a much

clearer knowledge on the part of managers, in particular, of the basis on which government and industry work in Britain. What are the real roots of political and industrial power and how is that power exercised? This difficult but necessary analysis will be the task of Chapter 2.

Chapter 2

GOVERNMENT AND INDUSTRY

Somehow politicians and businessmen have to learn to communicate more effectively and to work together in a way that makes proper allowance for the differing pressures under which they have to operate. If the problem is looked at from experience in both worlds, it must be recognised that many of the mistakes that have been made in recent years have, at least in part, sprung from genuine misunderstanding on both sides. The politician too often judges business to be motivated entirely by narrow self-interest and a desire to exploit government for its own financial ends. The businessman too often just fails to understand that the pressures on politicians are unique to political life and have no counterpart in industry.

THE CONSTITUTIONAL POSITION

There is one fact that must always be in the minds of those who would understand the workings of the British constitution. It is that the constitution is 'unwritten' and therefore based on a hotch-potch of history, fascinating to the student, but highly confusing to those who might believe it to be a code of conduct for governments. For example, the right of private members of the House of Commons to act against the executive still rests on the formal introduction, each session, of a bill never passed and originally intended to deal with outlaws in the King's 'New Forest'. No parliamentary bill can become a legally enforceable act until the Royal Assent has been signified in the words of the original Norman French, '*La Reine la veult.*' The proceedings of the House of Commons are governed by precedents from time to time laid down by successive 'Speakers' and enshrined in *Erskine May* (the reference book of previous Speakers' rulings); there are no other rules.

In case these instances may be regarded as the trappings and not the substance, it should be noted that cabinet government itself has no more precise foundation. It sprang from the Norman 'Curia Regis' which evolved into the Privy Council of Henry VI. Until the eighteenth century the Sovereign in Privy Council was the chief source of executive power in the state. After this date the powers of the Privy Council were slowly developed in the 'Cabinet', which was itself a committee of the Privy Council. Other Council committees evolved to become the ministries and departments of today.

Managers looking for parliamentary job specifications to guide them in the ways of Parliament and government are likely to remain confused. Yet the system works, and on the whole works well, within nineteenth-century parameters. Whether these are appropriate to the second half of the twentieth century is a matter for later discussion. At this stage it is only necessary to provide some clues to the understanding of the workings of the system as it now is. This understanding is a 'must' for managers in a society that has a large and increasing sector of state-owned or state-controlled industry.

THE POLITICAL MACHINE

The system is above all a power structure, and the most vital thing for anyone outside it is to know where the power resides and how it is exercised. To say that politics is about power and not really about anything else, is not to imply that politicians are motivated by the lust for power for its own sake. Politicians are much less complicated and much more honest and straightforward than their detractors would have us believe. Equally, civil servants are not the power-drugged mandarins that they are sometimes unfairly represented to be. The manager will have to deal with both classes of legislator. He will see more of the civil servants than of their political masters and very little, if anything, of the two figures who head the respective pyramids of power: the Prime Minister and the Head of the Civil Service. Yet this is where power begins and where a study of how to deal with the structure must start.

A Prime Minister has much more real power than those who have not been in politics realise. He exercises almost total power so long as he retains the support of his cabinet colleagues. His structure title is 'First Lord of the Treasury' and this is where his management power derives. The Treasury has steadily strengthened its hold on modern cabinets and governments, no doubt with the full support of successive Prime Ministers. It is a mandatory cabinet procedure that no policy paper can be put to Cabinet by any minister, involving expenditure, that has not first been cleared with the Treasury. So power clearly resides at No. 10 Downing Street. The Cabinet Office, staffed with the young élite of the Civil Service, together with the men in the top echelon of the Treasury, has the deciding voice. All this of course, is subject to the proceedings of the Cabinet itself. Cabinets can and do use their collective power when they debate contentious issues, but it would be a badly managed Cabinet that had to start counting heads, on all decisions, in any very obvious way. The Secretary of the Cabinet is no longer titular Head of the Civil Service, but he is still the next best thing to it. Cabinet minutes only record decisions of the Cabinet, normally the Prime Minister's summing up of debate and decision. A Prime Minister's personal minute, as Churchill demonstrated, is still the one overriding order that can condition the whole machinery of government.

From the point of view of business decision-making, no cabinet minister, however powerful he may be in his own right, can 'promise' or 'perform' without the support of the Cabinet, which effectively means the Prime Minister and the Treasury where expenditure is concerned. Most routine matters are, of course, disposed of departmentally within the overall policy laid down by the government. Often the particular minister himself is not involved, but the big policy decisions are subject to a long process of cabinet examination and debate. The proposals must come up through the ministry itself, a scenario of many episodes, until they reach the Civil Service head of the ministry, that is, the Permanent Secretary. From him they pass to the minister (clearance with the Treasury takes place at this stage), and then are submitted to the Cabinet. At this point, if the matter is complicated or contentious, it may get referred to one of the inner cabinet committees—'Home Affairs' or 'Defence', for example—where further time will be lost before it returns to the Cabinet. Finally, if the Cabinet approves, the cabinet-minute notes agreement and this is the signal for the ministry to proceed to implement. During this period, weeks or months may have passed and no one, including the minister, has any authority to act until it is 'through' Cabinet.

A bold, or sometimes a stupid, minister may try to short-circuit this procedure. Two common methods are: by making a commitment to the public or to Parliament that goes beyond cabinet authority, and by lobbying cabinet colleagues on a 'knock for knock' basis. Such action rarely endears a minister to his colleagues and, in any case, the whole Cabinet still has the final word. Obviously, on any matter of importance, any minister has the right of final appeal to the Cabinet; if he feels deeply enough he may back his case with at least an implied threat of resignation. This can be a risky procedure but it is sometimes inevitable, as I found out for myself when I was Minister of Transport in 1956. I could not persuade the Treasury and the then Chancellor of the Exchequer to provide the Ministry with adequate funds to enable it to go ahead with the five main road-construction projects that I had singled out for top priority treatment. These projects were the very minimum necessary to make any kind of start on a real road-building programme. So the Ministry had to register disagreement and take the problem to Cabinet as the final court of appeal. In

making my case I described to the Cabinet what I felt the
government had to do for the motorist, in somewhat uncompromising terms. I knew that I was playing it as forcefully as I
dared to my colleagues, all of whom had pet spending projects of their own. In the end I got the money, at the price of a
deserved reproof from Harold Macmillan who told the Cabinet,
quite fairly, that it was unusual for colleagues to address
demands to it in quite such peremptory tones.

This is just one example of how difficult it can be for a
minister to get enough of his own way in Cabinet to allow the
continuance of policies sponsored by his ministry. It follows
from this that, in judging the power of a ministry to get its
policies through, one has to know something of the status of
the minister in Cabinet and his capacity for influencing the
Prime Minister and his colleagues. Ministers of so-called
'Cabinet rank' who are not in the Cabinet, for example, start
with an almost hopeless disadvantage. As departmental
ministers, but not members of the Cabinet, they are summoned
to Cabinet at No. 10 at approximately the time that their own
business is likely to be taken. Then they have to await the
summons sitting outside the red baize door of the cabinet
room, in a small alcove off the main entrance hall of No. 10.
Here they are subject to all the comings and goings of officials
and other ministers also waiting their turn. When the summons
eventually comes, they are ushered abruptly into the cabinet
room, totally unaware of the mood of the meeting and often
hard put to it to even find a seat at the cabinet table.

It is a somewhat daunting procedure. A marble bust of the
Duke of Wellington stands above the fireplace which forms the
main feature of the 'cosy corner' made for waiting ministers.
His disdainful air does nothing to encourage their spirits and,
looking back, I am quite sure that unless I had achieved membership of the Cabinet under Harold Macmillan I should have
found the task of making enough money available for building
the new roads for Britain an impossible one. Junior ministers,
be they called Minister or Parliamentary Secretary, with all

respect to them, have no power at all. So managers seeking undertakings from ministers or their departments must make a careful assessment of what these are likely to be able to deliver.

THE MINISTER AND HIS OFFICIALS

So much for cabinet procedure. Many decisions that naturally affect business and management are taken within a ministry and need no cabinet sanction, because they fall within the orbit of existing government policy. So the relationships between the minister and his senior officials are important. It may also be that, in this sphere, the minister or Secretary of State will devolve more day-to-day decision making upon one of his junior ministerial colleagues. He cannot, of course, devolve the constitutional responsibility which is his alone and has no one to share it. If his ministry is in error, it is his head that Parliament and the public will rightly demand.

So relationships between a minister and his ministry often represent the difference between success or failure on the part of the minister. On first arriving at his ministry, a minister, following an appointment, is met on the front steps by the Permanent Secretary of his new ministry and conducted to his ministerial office. There, in the Minister's Office, he is introduced to the Principal and Assistant Private Secretaries, who have served his predecessor, even if he was of another party and another government. There is a story, that has more than a grain of truth in it, about an ambitious young minister who at this stage produced a piece of paper, handed it to the Permanent Secretary and said, 'There, Permanent Secretary, are the five major things that I wish to do during my period as Minister.' The Permanent Secretary at that point also produced a piece of paper from his pocket, handed it to the minister with a smile and said, 'And there, Minister, are five reasons which show quite conclusively why none of your five projects are possible of attainment.'

Ministers must strive never to be the prisoners of their ministries; rather they must be a constant source of new ideas which their advisers can shape and fashion against the whetstone of the collective wisdom of their department. The British Civil Service is the finest administrative machine in the world but, by very reason of its long and noble traditions, it is there primarily to administer and not to create. Even today it has not been fully immersed in the cut and thrust of business practice. It is therefore inevitably biased towards a negative rather than a positive approach. Its duty is to warn, to counsel, to make sure that its ministers do not get themselves into dire trouble in the House of Commons or the country. In this protective role it is bound to say 'no' more often than 'yes'. It is ministers therefore, and not ministries, who must provide the spur.

An increasing danger of modern political life, with all its press of detail and spread of responsibility in government, is that ministers too often just do not have the opportunity to think around the problems and thus try to see the wood as well as the trees. They are normally grossly overworked and a typical ministerial day could well be something like the following:

0900   Arrive Minister's Office. Deal with urgent departmental work.
1100   Cabinet meeting at No. 10.
1300   Official lunch.
1430   Question time at the House of Commons.
1530–2200   Committee stage of bill or involvement in debate. See officials in own ministerial room in House of Commons in between times to try and catch up with work. If House rises punctually, which it rarely does, complete work at Ministry if necessary.
After 2200   Home to read at least one despatch box full of telegrams, cabinet papers and other documents—one to two hours' work for even a rapid reader.
Around 2400   Inevitable press calls, either through the

ministry, or directly if Fleet Street has the minister's
number, as it usually has.

0100   Sleep, if possible.

That for many ministers would be a very lightly stressed day;
many other horrors could be added to taste: business depu-
tations, for example!

Civil servants are often as hard worked, but obviously not as
publicly exposed, as ministers. As they are very conscious of the
strains on their minister, it need not cause surprise if they
sometimes seek to shelter him from those who could often give
him useful advice. The power structure of the official side of a
ministry is again pyramidic in form, with the Permanent
Secretary or Under Secretary at its apex. He, not the minister,
is the official head of the ministry, and it is the Permanent
Secretary who is the accounting officer. It is thus the Permanent
Secretary or his deputies who answer to the Public Accounts
Committee and other monitoring bodies set up by Parliament
to interrogate ministers outside the scope of the parliamentary
question.

Parliamentary questions can be the bane of a busy minister's
existence. Question time in the House of Commons is often the
kind of free-for-all that makes managers despair of ever understanding politics. Yet the basic proposition is a simple one.
It is to provide a parliamentary check on the executive, by
making it answerable in detail to Parliament. Each ministry
takes its turn on set days and, as more than one ministry has to
be allocated to one day and all questions are not reached
orally, each ministry slowly creeps up the batting order on its
question day, until it is top of the list and thus bound to have
to answer orally. Then the minister had better look out, if his
ministry has problems. The ministry provides its minister with
the first formal answer to the question and a much longer
brief covering points that it thinks the questioner may want to
raise as supplementary questions, if the Speaker allows them.
At this point the minister is on his own; no one can brief him

or help him at this stage. He must answer or be howled down
and his answer must be pertinent, factual, serious, humorous,
sharp, soothing, positive or negative as he judges necessary in
the seconds that he has to decide as he rises to reply, often to a
long barrage of interruptions. If he gets it right he acquires
much honour; if he stumbles, then even some of his colleagues
behind him will not hesitate to put in the debating 'boot'.

These examples are perhaps enough to demonstrate that the
rules of the game in politics cannot easily be equated with those
in business. Democracy is not a 'yes' or 'no' business. It
encompasses a highly volatile and qualified area of skilled
personal judgements that lie entirely outside the experience of
most managers and businessmen.

It should be possible to find ways of bringing government and
industry more closely together, and solutions to this problem
must be part of any viable strategy for industrial survival.
The problem is not, however, entirely one of seeking to make
politics conform to business; this would be to assume, quite
unfairly, that failures in collaboration have always been the
fault of the politicians. Industry's refusal to seek to understand
the democratic imperative, or even to be willing to accept that
such a force exists, is equally to blame. Industry could also be
held blameworthy for an unwillingness to accept that its own
circumstances have suffered many changes since 1945, both
in Britain and in the markets of the world. These changes and
the operating circumstances arising from them need understanding, in just the same way as do the problems of modern
politics. Only on the basis of a fair assessment of the problems
of both sides could proposals for working more fruitfully
together be put forward.

THE CHANGED WORLD OF BUSINESS

Business remained personal and autocratic long after politics
had become a matter of consensus. Large corporations built
by one man are still recognisable as are their products. Morris

or Ford in the automobile business, Selfridge or Fraser in retailing, Sopwith, or Douglas in aerospace, are only a few names. Some family business dynasties continue—such as the Rockefellers', the Siefs' and the Rothschilds'—but personal control of a vast business is today rare enough to be a misleading exception. Business today in Britain, Europe or the USA has to conform to its own particular style of business democracy. It is in general owned by shareholders, managed by professional managers and operated by employees who are, more likely than not, organised in some power grouping which is wider in scope than the individual business. The old mythologies of two sides of industry—that is, the boss and his workers, or the necessity for trade unions as a bulwark against sweated labour and crude exploitation—should long ago have disappeared. The fact that many industrial practices that belong to the early nineteenth century are still being talked about in the last half of the twentieth century is proof that business too has its clouded areas of misunderstanding and misconception.

The fact is that the postwar years have been more than an era of revolutionary change in the relationship between government and industry and in the degree of government intervention in industry. Change has not stopped there. The relationships between managers and employees, and the whole scale and pattern of industrial development, have been similarly revolutionised. Entry into Europe has added another powerful impetus to further change. In the light of these circumstances, it is perhaps not surprising that there has arisen in all industrialised societies a mood of sharp questioning about the objectives of commerce and industry. As Britain, in particular, is today a business-centred society, with free enterprise providing the majority of all jobs and the 100 largest companies producing over 50 per cent of net output, it is inevitable that the free enterprise system and the profit motive that sustains it should be the focus of much of this questioning. Business has criticised politicians and academics; in return, many in political and academic life have led the way in challenging the objectives of business and the quality of life at which it aims. They have challenged: the opportunities that it offers, particularly to the young; its economic and social policies, which are often held to divide the social fabric; the inequality of wealth and the undesirability of profits; the size of modern business organisation (particularly the so-called multinationals); and, above all, the relationship of the modern business to its employees and its shareholders.

The Economist's Intelligence Unit summarised the scene as it saw it at the commencement of 1975, in these words:

'. . . the private sector in this country is currently under unprecedented scrutiny. Capitalism, and its claim as the fairest and most effective vehicle for the creation and distribution of wealth, is now being subjected to a stern re-examination, not only by those of the Left who have always been hostile, but also amongst the uncommitted who see a need for re-assessment. For very many people under 35 years of age, the anti-capitalist view of highly diversified, multi-national corporations exerting unacceptable pressure on governments, consumers, markets and prices, to the sole benefit of their shareholders and themselves, contains a large ingredient of truth, however much Business may protest that such a view is a grotesque misrepresentation of the real situation.'

Business and its managers may indeed protest, like politicians, that they are misrepresented and misunderstood. This may indeed be so, but it does not alter the fact that the free enterprise business-orientated way of life is increasingly being challenged. Perhaps many of the challengers do not wish to be unduly confused with the facts. Some of them, in any case, desire to pull down the house of capitalism in its entirety. Notwithstanding this, much more needs to be done to make the facts about modern business available to those who want to know them. Possible changes in the structure of modern business will be a matter for later discussion. It is the purpose of this chapter to set out some of the parameters that govern present-day business operations. It is fair to comment that business operates today in a much more socially conscious fashion than many of its detractors would have us believe. But the growth in social awareness has sprung, not so much from the present structure of free enterprise, as from the beliefs of a new genera-tion of directors and managers whose view is that this structure has to change.

The framework of today's limited liability company is not all that different from what it was before the 1939–45 war (or, for that matter, the 1914–18 war). Behind the facade great changes have taken place, particularly as far as shareholders are concerned. Today over 50 per cent of shares in industry are held by 'institutions'. These include pension funds (among which are the funds of nationalised industries and local authorities), insurance companies, investment trust companies, unit trusts and charitable trusts. In other words, the majority owner of the British public company is no longer the private shareholder; rather it is a series of corporate bodies which owe their first allegiance not to the company in which they hold shares, but to their own shareholders in their own fund or trust. This divided control has tended in the postwar years to remove from boards of directors at least some of the useful spur to action that can be provided by the questioning and probing of individual shareholders. To 'sell and go away' may be the right way for an institution to act with regard to the shares it holds in a company which it fears may be in trouble. This may well be in the short-term interests of its own shareholders, but it is not in the longer-term interests of British industry.

The boards of the larger companies where institutional holdings are paramount have therefore been subjected to a different and, in some ways, less pressing discipline from their shareholders. Meantime the larger companies have been getting larger by merger, acquisition and growth, until today some 100 large companies dominate British industry. This situation is no different from that in Europe or America, and over the whole trading area of the free world it is the international or multinational companies that have grown largest and fastest. In Britain today, multinationals provide over 70 per cent of the nation's exports. It is a strange paradox, however, that those who criticise the growth in size and power of the multinational company usually support the growth of a largely British phenomenon, namely, nationalised industry. Many of Britain's competitors have state-owned industry, but only in Britain has the growth of nationalised industry remained an area of acute political controversy. Whatever views one may hold on the desirability or otherwise of nationalisation or denationalisation, there can be little doubt that much of what has gone wrong in Britain in the postwar years stems from emphasis on nationalisation or denationalisation as a political act, to the exclusion of management considerations. Many of the nation's industrial troubles have arisen from disputes originating in nationally owned industries. The government has not succeeded in avoiding direct involvement in industrial strife in this area, despite the fact that the nationalised statutes themselves do not allow this. Moreover, the government's direct interference in the conduct of nationalised industries has led to growing government involvement in and interference with industry as a whole. Nor has the nationalisation concept done much to pioneer better human relations within industry; in fact, it has often done the very opposite. Nationalised industry has been the breeding ground for confrontation between the government and trade unions over the last twenty years. Added to this, the unfortunate irrelevance of much of the Conservative Industrial Relations Act 1971 and of the Socialist 'in place of strife' initiative has made the industrial relations scene an even darker one, where in many areas the abuse of power has led to industrial strife rather than to co-operation and participation. Meantime, in Western Europe bold experiments have been initiated particularly in West Germany where so-called 'worker directors' have achieved board membership, although in a context inapplicable to present British company structure. In a more general context, the original members of the European Economic Community have been working hard for many years now to reform and restructure their business organisations. This fact alone presents British business with a new challenge, and we have underestimated the management effort that will be required to equate British and European business practice and thus to lay the foundations for an EEC code of business practice and conduct which will be binding on all its members.

So the postwar British business scene is unstructured and confused. The elements of beneficent change are present, but so are those of almost total disruption. As a legacy of the past we have complacently believed British industrial relations to lead the world. In a similar position we have believed British industry to be strong enough and prosperous enough to stand the immense strains of politically motivated change through the nationalisation statutes. As a result the present situation is totally unsatisfactory. British industry today is in danger of becoming an incompatible mixture of state and free enterprise. British industrial relations are in a mess and many European countries are now ahead of Britain in developments in this area. In the league tables of growth and efficiency Britain nudges Italy for bottom place. So again the question 'What has gone wrong?' has to be asked. Clearly, the major adverse factor is the distortion of the postwar market economy by increasing government intervention and interference. This has been imposed first indirectly through an increasing programme of nationalisation and now more directly through the imposition of the National Enterprise Board, planning agreements and other devices.

So it is at the interface between government and industry in particular that, in the postwar years, the scale of operations has been wrong, human relations have been muddled and non-viable relationships between government and industry have been created.

This is the real challenge to managers, whether they work in government or in private enterprise. If Britain is to prosper the area of incompatibility has to be reduced, so as to create at least the possibility of an on-going practical dialogue in the national interest between government and industry leading to agreement on respective spheres of influence.

Chapter 3

THE PROBLEM OF SCALE AND RELATIONSHIP: THE CASE OF THE BRITISH AEROSPACE INDUSTRY

Let us now turn to some practical examples of the problems of scale and size that have beset British industry in the postwar period. These are best examined in the context of a case study of the aerospace industry. From British experience in this area can be drawn some painful and precise examples of what needs to be done to avoid future error. This industry is Britain's largest exporter of high technology products. Its conversion rate of raw materials to finished products is favourable. Its innovations and technology have been outstanding. Yet an examination of its history over three decades provides a continuous record of missed opportunities. During this period, circumstances have provided me with personal contacts with the industry as a machine tool manufacturer, as Minister of Civil Aviation and then of Defence and latterly once again as an industrialist. It is from these various points of view that this study is constructed.

First, some case history illustrative of the risks of being involved in a 'battle of the giants' with the USA aerospace industry will be presented. Some of the evidence may be twenty years old—but Britain is still having to live with the results. This is a lesson in itself on the problems of scale.

THE BATTLE OF THE 'BLUE RIBAND'
In the early 1950s it was becoming clear that the 'blue riband of the Atlantic', as it had passed from sail to steam, was now to

pass from the ocean to the air. The aircraft that won the race for the prestige crossing of the North Atlantic from Europe to the USA would be in a strong position to dominate the air routes of the world.

Thanks to a brilliant initiative by Sir George Edwards and his design team at Vickers, Britain secured a lead in the medium-range passenger-aircraft field with the Viscount turbo-prop aircraft. This aircraft became the main support of all the European operations of British European Airways, but it did not have the range for the Atlantic. Here it looked originally as if the race would be won by the de Havilland Comet jet passenger aircraft, which was Britain's only entrant in the long-haul jet race. But the Americans were developing a much broader range of jet aircraft based on their wartime experience. Leading the field here was a development of the American KC135, that is, a four-jet tanker aircraft developed for the US Air Force with most of the initial proving and research costs supported by the US Air Force vote. This was to be the test bed from which the Boeing 707 passenger aircraft would be developed. Meantime, in actual passenger service the long-range requirement was being met by the last generation of piston engine aircraft, such as the Douglas DC7C, and by turbo-prop aircraft of greater capacity and larger range than the Viscount. All these aircraft, turbo-prop or pure jet, had sprung from an original British concept, namely the 'Whittle' jet engine.

Then, without warning, the whole Comet programme was halted by the failure of the aircraft fuselage to withstand the immense stresses of flying at over 30,000 feet at jet speeds. The gamble on Britain's first and only long-range passenger jet had failed. Britain then proceeded, by a long process of public inquiry, to publish the failure to the world and to educate American competitors as to what not to do when designing airframes for jet altitudes and speeds. Against this background a letter that I wrote in 1955, as a junior government minister in the Ministry of Labour to the then Minister of Supply, sums up the problem as the industry saw it at this time. The Britannia was a long-range turbo-prop aircraft, of which more later in this chapter; the V1060 was a four jet passenger derivative of the Vickers jet bomber aircraft; and the Comet IV was the strengthened fuselage version of the Comet Mark I.

'Firstly, there seems to be a general feeling that we are going to miss the boat on the North Atlantic service. The possible aircraft here are thought to be the long range Britannia and the Vickers 1000. Information seems to be mixed about the Britannia as far as the Atlantic service is concerned but, in any case, I imagine that a prop jet on this kind of service cannot compete with a pure jet which obviously must take the blue riband. Rumour has it that the Vickers 1000 is going to be rejected by the RAF as too complicated, and that as the company is not really enthusiastic about adding the new aircraft to their existing heavy commitments, the project must fall to the ground. As there is nothing on the stocks beyond the Comet IV, this would leave us with no jet passenger aircraft capable of competing in the North Atlantic service. An additional difficulty which is foreseen is that unless RAF Transport Command can have some long range jet aircraft (the Comet II is not the answer to this), we are not building up a reserve of trained pilots who can handle this kind of aircraft. If the above is correct, while we may hold markets for the short range aircraft such as the Viscount and the predominantly Commonwealth routes with the Britannia and Comet IV, the outlook for the North Atlantic prestige service seems very poor, and this must surely have an adverse effect on our aircraft sales and on our competitive position with the American aircraft industry.'

No doubt there seemed to be conclusive reasons at the time why this particular project for the jet passenger aircraft could not have been carried forward, but it left Britain committed to maintaining the North Atlantic service with the Britannia, an aircraft which was dependent on engines originally designed for flying boats! Trouble was inevitable.

Then I was appointed Minister of Civil Aviation and in September 1957 I had the difficult task of advising the Prime Minister that it was not acceptable for the Queen to travel to the United States and Canada in a British Britannia aircraft of the British Overseas Airways Corporation. Ostensibly the decision had to be presented on the basis that crew training and proving flights for this important new passenger aircraft were not completed. But, in fact, the problems were much deeper than this, as my following minute shows. The DC7C aircraft had been bought by BOAC from the US Douglas Company to bridge the gap left by the Comet failure.

'Regretfully I must advise that the use of a Britannia aircraft by Her Majesty the Queen on her forthcoming visit to the United States and Canada is quite impossible. Fortunately we can take this decision on grounds other than the difficulties with the engine of this aircraft which I deal with below.

'BOAC only took delivery yesterday of their first long range Britannia. They will not receive the second before mid October and it is of course essential to have two aircraft for this operation, one being a standby. In addition of course there is the fact that no chance has been given for a programme of proving flights or crew training, so I think we can safely let the decision rest on that. Air Commodore Sir Edward Fielding will, I understand, be advising Her Majesty in a similar sense.

'The choice therefore lies between two types of American aircraft which BOAC regularly use on their transatlantic flights. These are the Douglas DC7C and the Boeing Stratocruiser. Of these the Douglas is more up to date and is capable of non-stop flight in both directions. It is a well tried and thoroughly proved aircraft in the service of the Corporation and I therefore recommend that Her Majesty be humbly advised to travel in a DC7C. I append some notes on this aircraft in case you should find them useful. This decision has been widely forecast in the Press and therefore will not I hope add further adverse comments to the Britannia story.

'I think, however, you should know the facts about the Britannia which are causing BOAC and my Ministry a great deal of anxiety. The aircraft has of course the normal teething troubles that one expects with any new type but unfortunately its Proteus engine has developed major icing troubles. These are partly due to the design of the air intake and will therefore be more difficult to cure. At first it was thought that the trouble arose only from one kind of ice, known as "dry ice" and at least a partial cure was found for this. Unfortunately troubles are now arising from the more normal "wet ice" which of course is found over a much wider area and in more normal flying conditions. The Corporation and my Ministry have kept closely in touch with the Ministry of Supply and as a result some months ago, Dr Gardner of the Royal Aircraft Establishment was appointed as head of an expert committee which has been working very hard on all the possible solutions to this problem.

'There is no doubt that there is no final cure to this problem at the moment except a redesign of the engine intake which would take probably two years, so our only hope is to press on and try every possible kind of modification in the hope that this will make the engine acceptable in normal route flying.'

I had escaped ministerial responsibility for the extremely difficult situation that arose from the Comet crashes, as these had happened in the time of my predecessors in office. But I was to inherit the aftermath of British airlines' trying to maintain first-class air services around the world in competition with the Americans, on the basis of equipment that was inadequate to the task in hand. I set out the problems, as I saw

them, in a further minute to the Prime Minister on 24 June
1958:

'I was at this time on the point of suggesting to my
colleagues that a number of urgent problems facing us in
civil aviation required the attention of Ministers, the fare
structure being but one of them. On further reflection I am
convinced that all these problems should be considered
together. Before I suggest how this should be done I should
perhaps outline a few of the questions I have in mind.

'First, you will remember how hard we tried to reverse the
Australian and New Zealand decisions to buy Lockheed
Electra aircraft in place of a British type. Our failure was
largely due to the uneconomic terms on which Lockheeds
were prepared to buy back Constellation aircraft against the
sale of Electras. This situation may well repeat itself all over
the world and it is the measure of the competition that we
face for the Britannia and the Vanguard. Yet if Vickers fail
to sell any more Vanguards they will lose £8–10m.

'Looking further into the future, we face the problem of
producing a supersonic passenger transport aircraft to
follow the VC10. Here again many difficulties arise and,
although a joint study of this project is at the moment being
carried out by a number of firms, I fear that the present
effort is being dissipated so widely that progress is unlikely
to be sufficiently rapid.

'Another question is: should we back the Fairey Rotodyne?
I believe this might be a world-beating aircraft like the
Viscount, but it is new and untried; BEA, probably rightly,
feel at the moment that they cannot place an order. Also, the
future of any Canberra replacement is bound up with civil
aircraft because this might be a project which would lead to
a supersonic civil aircraft. Then there has been the recent
discussion about the Barnes Wallis movable wing aircraft
and there is Short Brothers' vertical-lift project, both of
which need study.

'It may be said that these things fall within the scope of the Padmore Committee. Whilst I am quite sure that the Padmore Committee will do an invaluable job, it cannot be expected to take difficult policy decisions which are the responsibility of the Ministers concerned. There is a problem here too for, as the industry swings over from the largely military to largely civil commitments, all our departmental responsibilities are getting more interdependent. The problem of differential fares is a good example of this.

'I think therefore that there is an unassailable case for finding a convenient way of co-ordinating policy between the Air Ministry, the Ministry of Supply, the Board of Trade, my own Ministry and the Treasury.

'It is my firm conviction that unless we take steps of this kind quickly we shall not only face great difficulties with our aircraft industry at home, but we shall also lose our present position in the export of aircraft and aircraft engines.'

If the Prime Minister had provided a means of co-ordinating policy in the way I had suggested, we might have got some of the problems solved. But this would have implied subordination of the political argument to arguments of a business and commercial nature. Even so, the proposal seems much more relevant than the current decision to increase rather than decrease the political element.

THE POLITICAL ISSUES

However, it was perhaps natural at that time that ministers should be more involved in arguments about whether BOAC and BEA (a) should be nationalised or denationalised, and (b) if nationalised, should be run solely in the interests of a profit-making airline, or solely in the interests of the British aircraft industry, or in a mixture of both sets of interests. The situation was further complicated by a natural desire on the part of the Conservative Party to encourage competition in the British airline business by providing opportunities for shipping companies to set up their own airlines and thus to share in the steady move of passenger and freight traffic from the ocean to the air. So continuing political arguments distracted attention from the real issues, which were how to carry more passengers by British airlines and how to sell more British aircraft to foreign airlines as well as to BOAC and BEA. To achieve both aims concentration should have been placed on developing the pure jet carrier, using the V1000 as a second runner to the Comet, and not on trying to achieve success in the long-range field with the turbo-prop, despite its dramatic success through the Viscount in the medium-range field.

After the Comet failure, with no pure jet successor there was no alternative but to try to make a success of the Britannia, but one can imagine the strains on BOAC as it competed with other major world airlines under these circumstances. In the end, with all the difficulties of the Britannia and with the failure to produce a satisfactory jet successor to the Comet, BOAC had to be allowed to buy fifteen Boeing 707 passenger jet aircraft to maintain itself in business. The only concession that could be made to the British aerospace industry was that these aircraft had to be fitted with Rolls-Royce engines. This deal may have inadvertently started another heresy which has bedevilled the British aerospace industry, namely that it would be possible to combine a viable British aero-engine industry with a foreign, normally American, airframe industry. Subsequent events have certainly proved that a satisfactory aerospace industry must rest on an adequate airframe as well as adequate engine capacity. BOAC was very grateful for this decision. It was only natural that, after all its problems with the Comet, then with the Britannia, there should be a strong 'buy American' school within the corporation.

At this time in the mid 1950s it was not surprising that, as a result of these events, the equipment situation in British airlines was confused. For example, BEA in 1956–7 had a staff of some 10,000. The Corporation had sixty-three Viscount turbo-prop aircraft and was just about to take delivery of twenty of the larger turbo-prop Vanguards, which would each seat about 130 passengers. BEA was also committed to six Comet IVs as interim aircraft to meet jet competition on its routes. The first of the de Havilland Trident aircraft, the DH121, was still seven or eight years away.

BOAC employed some 19,000 people. It had a very mixed bag of aircraft, namely 32 Britannias, 8 Comet IVs with 11 more to come, and 10 DC7Cs. It was expecting delivery of the 15 Boeing 707s and, some six or seven years away, delivery of 35 VC10 jet aircraft which at that time were scheduled primarily for BOAC's African and Australian routes. In the armed forces a Canberra replacement was becoming increasingly urgent and with the Fairey Rotodyne and the Hawker Siddeley P1127 vertical lift jet it was possible to consider moving into the short take-off area.

I felt, both as Minister of Civil Aviation and later as Minister of Defence, that there was a need for a businessman's approach to the rationalisation of equipment for the two air corporations and for the armed forces. Out of this rationalisation I hoped to achieve a soundly based airline and aerospace industry. The first problem was a jet replacement, namely a short- and medium-haul aircraft for BEA. This decision provides a useful case history of the tensions that can arise under the British system of nationalisation between the chairman of a nationalised industry and his minister.

Lord Sholto Douglas was the Chairman of BEA. I liked Sholto. In my view he was doing a very good job of leading BEA, with the extremely able support of Tony Milward, his chief executive. We got on well together, but BEA's requirements for a European jet aircraft were so tightly and—it is only fair to say—expertly drawn by BEA technicians that my Ministry of Civil Aviation and the Ministry of Supply both believed that the aircraft that BEA wanted would have little or no sales appeal to other airlines whose route requirements needed a more flexible configuration. Matters came to a head at a meeting between Sholto Douglas and myself with our various officials. He looked me straight in the eye and said, 'Minister, if you are prepared to prefer the judgement of your advisers to mine and you will give me a letter directing me to purchase an aircraft which is not of my choice, I will be happy to accept your direction, but I shall, of course, feel it necessary to publish your letter.' Needless to say Sholto Douglas won, as he probably should have done. It is equally true to say that what he wanted has proved to be fundamentally right for BEA. But my Ministry was equally right, for the Trident has not sold well to other competing airlines and, except in China, did not allow the British aerospace industry to establish itself in the world market for tri-jet rear engine aircraft.

Whether it was right to refuse to override the Chairman of BEA, to the detriment of the wider interests of the British aerospace industry, is an issue which is symptomatic of the extreme difficulty of achieving satisfactory business relations between a Minister and the chairman of a nationalised industry, when major commercial policy is involved. Blurred responsibilities always arise. **Is the prior responsibility political and thus to Parliament, or is it commercial and thus to the financial success of the corporation— or of the industry—and who decides? The requirements seldom coincide.** So a minister is pulled two ways. As minister he answers for the corporation to Parliament, but he has little power over its day-to-day decisions, which are taken by the industry's own board. So even if good personal relations exist between the minister and the chairman there is a policy tug of war all the way down the line between the minister and the corporation. **What a way to run what are essentially highly competitive businesses!**

Relationships between BOAC and the Ministry of Civil Aviation were also very involved in the discussions that led to the placing of a contract for the Vickers VC10 with what is now the British Aircraft Corporation. It was only too understandable that, after the traumas of the Comet and the Britannia, BOAC would feel strongly motivated towards buying American aircraft. Indeed it had already made a fairly major switch to US equipment in terms of the DC7C and then the Boeing 707. From its point of view this position was only too understandable, but it seemed to me and my advisers to be a policy that might well put the British airframe industry out of business. The sort of discussion that went on is perhaps best summarised by a short letter which I wrote to Gerard d'Erlanger, then Chairman of BOAC, in June 1956:

'I am writing in confirmation of my telephone message of this afternoon. de Havillands gave me to understand when I was with them today that there was quite a chance that by, say, 1961, they could produce an aircraft not much slower than the big American jets with a passenger capacity of perhaps a little under 100 and a runway requirement of 6 to 7,000 feet. If they can do this, it will clearly be a fact which will need very serious consideration in deciding upon your future aircraft requirements. While the large American jets might still hold the advantage on the specialised North Atlantic routes, I should have thought that an aircraft of this sort of performance would—setting aside altogether the fact that it is British—be a preferable commercial proposition for operations in the rest of the world.

'de Havillands also told me that BOAC had not yet made any serious attempt to evaluate what they (de Havillands) could make for them. I think you agreed with me when we spoke that, now that you are sending a technical mission to the United States, it is most important that there can be no cause for complaint that similar opportunity was not given to British manufacturers to show what they could produce. We therefore agreed that you would take immediate steps to see that BOAC and de Havillands get together on this matter and go thoroughly into it.

'I shall be very interested to hear what emerges from these talks.'

In the end it was not de Havilland that got the order but Vickers, with their concept of a large passenger aircraft with tail mounted engines and an outstanding runway performance. Here again there were problems over policy. BOAC was really only willing to accept a British aircraft for some of its other world routes. On the prestigious North Atlantic run it proposed to continue to fly American. So the specification for the VC10 was a somewhat warped one from the very beginning. Yet for the sake of the British aerospace industry, Britain had to get back into the large passenger aircraft business. So I wrote again to the Chairman of BOAC in October 1956, acknowledging a formal letter of thanks from the corporation on the purchase of the Boeing 707s and saying again what I believed was the right policy both for BOAC and for the British airframe industry:

'Thank you for your letter of 25th October conveying the Board's appreciation of my support for your purchase of Boeing 707 aircraft. This, as you know, has not been an easy deal to arrange. It is certainly not one that we can repeat, as I am sure that you and your colleagues on the Board fully understand. What we have got to do now is first exploit our current generation of aircraft to the maximum possible extent, and we must all hope that the concerted action now being taken on the Britannia will get it flying in route service quickly.

'I hope too that every effort will be made to bring forward the Comet IVs as quickly as possible. Then we must succeed in our task of getting de Havillands to build for us an aircraft that is superior and more flexible than the Boeing for the purposes for which we require it. I cannot accept that a mere copy of the Boeing at this stage is of any use to BOAC and it would certainly not sell in world markets. Equally I cannot accept that, with all our current knowledge of the Boeing, we cannot now produce an aircraft that is better for our purposes and thus more saleable in the world.

'My support has, therefore, only enabled you to make a start in the task of taking a very much larger share of the world's air passenger traffic. I know that you are determined to succeed and I send to you and your colleagues my very best wishes in what will be a tough and challenging assignment.'

In the end BOAC ordered the VC10. Immediately the public announcement was made, the other side of the argument was taken up: Was the VC10 up to specification? Was it better than the Boeing or the Douglas? Ministers were soon deeply involved in the usual public arguments about the viability of any new British project in this sensitive area. It seemed that before any advanced project made in Britain worked, it became obsolete in terms of public relations. Certainly the Americans were much better at handling aerospace public relations than were the British. Soon the question was posed: Was it a money maker for BOAC or would the corporation have some case for subsidy, if it could be shown that the aircraft was more expensive in terms of cost per seat mile than were its American competitors? So the inevitable problem that faced every advanced British project in the air was arrived at. Britain could not afford to enter more than one horse in the race; therefore that horse had to be a certain winner, for if any trouble occurred there was no alternative runner available. The VC10 was also a good example of the dangers of the highly critical attitude of many British commentators towards new aerospace projects developed on this inevitable 'one-off' basis. In fact, BOAC was provided with an aircraft, in the VC10, that would, if all had gone well, have bridged the gap between the subsonic and supersonic jets, very much to the advantage of the corporation and thus of the British aerospace industry. It was only natural that the aircraft had its initial teething troubles—all aircraft do. These were not due to safety factors but because, as it later turned out, the aircraft needed minor modification to the attack angle of its rear engines if it was to provide a com-

petitive cost per seat mile. Because marketing techniques were
not at that time sufficiently advanced in BOAC, the fact that the
much greater comfort and quietness of this aircraft would attract
passengers from all over the world was largely overlooked.
So, sadly enough, in the end this great aircraft had a somewhat
lukewarm launch and, because it was not marketed in the right
way, it never fully met the hopes that everyone, including the
manufacturers, had for it. Indeed the political arguments
about whether BOAC should have been compensated for the
so-called shortcomings of this aircraft, in terms of operating
costs, went on long after I left the government. In fact, this
was one of the subjects dealt with in a report from a select
committee of the Commons, two years after I had returned to
business life. Meantime, BOAC had invested heavily in
Boeing 'jumbo' jets (747).

The underlying explanation of a highly unsatisfactory
situation was basically the inability on the part of ministers,
the Airline Chairmen's Committee and the British aerospace
industry to decide what the priorities really were. Was the top
priority the political one of 'making a commercial success of
nationalised industries'—the Conservative version—or one of
'giving them untrammelled support in the national interest
and a monopoly'—the socialist version? As governments
changed, so instructions to airline chairmen were reinterpreted,
if not totally changed. This led to confusion about how operating losses should be dealt with and whether there should be
capital write-offs, or subsidies, or some other way of satisfying
the needs of Parliament.

There were other problems within the aerospace industry
itself. The aero-engine manufacturers, led by Rolls-Royce, were
too inclined to assume that Britain could have a viable aero-
engine industry without necessarily having a viable British
airframe industry. Others regarded the two as complementary
to one another and subsequent events have proved that this
philosophy was right. However, it is not the purpose of this
study to say who was personally right or wrong. Probably

everyone concerned was both right and wrong at different times, and this goes for governments as well as airline chairmen of the industry. Everyone did his best and his duty as he saw it, but *the inevitable conclusion forced by the facts, is that those involved made their decisions within the wrong frame of reference.* It should have been possible to use the airline corporations as a showcase for the British aircraft industry, without unduly interfering with the corporations' airline operations. As the Viscount has proved for BEA, these two objectives were not necessarily incompatible. Unless the British aerospace industry had recourse to an order from one of the airline corporations, it had no hope at all of achieving the 80 or 100 aircraft off the production line which it was necessary to achieve, even in those days, to recover the initial costs of tooling-up and of producing and flight proving the first few prototype aircraft.

Therefore, postwar experience of this exciting but very politically charged sector of British industry has made it almost the perfect test case to show how difficult it is, within the framework of the British democratic system, to combine successful private enterprise with government intervention and control. Experience has supported the view that the true criticism of state intervention is concerned not only with political theory but also with the way state industries have been run. The concept of a mixed economy where nationalisation is supposed to exist as a kind of hybrid form of capitalism may have been right, but the actual operating situation, as experience has shown, has led only to the achievement of the worst aspects of both the state and the free enterprise methods of industrial control. Because of all these differing strands of political, airline and industrial policy, Britain missed a number of chances of establishing itself in this field and certainly missed the chance of achieving total success on a world basis for the best subsonic jet aircraft available in the 1960s, namely the VC10. *The lesson surely is that government must draw back from detailed intervention in industry, whether state or privately financed.*

THREE CASE STUDIES

This chapter would not be complete without a consideration of three other aviation projects, all of which have had a somewhat chequered career. Each story illuminates a different aspect of the problems of policy management in state industry.

The P1127: A Thirteen-Year Prototype
The P1127, the first vertical take-off aircraft without rotary wings, was a very advanced concept pioneered by Hawker Siddeley and its advanced teams of brilliant scientists and technicians. Here Britain had something quite unique. It obviously had a great deal to contribute to the Royal Air Force and to the strike and reconnaissance capability of the alliance of the North Atlantic Treaty Organisation. Also, within its overall concept lay the possibility of a solution to the vexed question of a joint aircraft for the Royal Air Force and the Fleet Air Arm. This aircraft concept was the ministerial responsibility of the Minister of Defence. The manufacturing agency was the Ministry of Supply. The minute which I sent, as Minister of Defence, to the then Minister of Supply in November 1959 sets out some of the problems and the hopes of using this project as a method of encouraging NATO joint arms projects.

'Thank you for your letter of 10th November about the P1127.
'I had already been taking an interest in the P1127 which seems a most promising line of development. I fully support the arrangements which have been agreed on between officials with the objective of harmonising the two requirements. I understand that this is already in hand.
'I doubt if we can go far in deciding our later course of action until NATO discussions have made some progress. When the Working Party meets we should try to steer it towards a project that can use the BS53 engine, and if possible

one that would make use of the experience gained with the P1127 and that might serve the purposes of the Royal Air Force, even though they are somewhat different. When we can see what kind of project is likely to materialise in NATO, we can decide whether it would suit us better to use the product for our own purposes or develop something different. This will depend partly on the characteristics of the NATO aircraft, and partly on how it is proposed to organise and pay for its development and production.

'Meanwhile the Treasury have already agreed, as I understand it, to enough money being put behind the P1127 in 1959/60 and 1960/61 to ensure that it goes ahead as fast as possible. I note that you are examining ways in which the development and production of an operational aircraft might be accelerated later. I should be grateful if you could keep me informed about this, both because of the potential importance of this class of aircraft and because when the question arises of the Government's assuming larger commitments, I shall need to consider carefully what it is that defence interests justify.'

As a result, as Minister of Defence, I soon found myself in the business of arms salesman, for it seemed obvious that unless West German and American support could be obtained for this prototype aircraft, the Ministry would not be able to justify to the Treasury the very large development cost (in those days some £50 million) of the airframe and engine. The industry was, in any case, working fairly near the frontiers of science at this time. Nobody had ever made an aircraft that could take off vertically by the thrust of its own jet engines, hover and then, by altering the direction of thrust, move forwards and operate as a conventional aircraft. It is a considerable tribute to the will to co-operate at that stage on behalf of the then Minister of Defence for West Germany, and the Secretary of Defense of the United States, that, in the end, agreement was achieved on a tripartite order for eighteen of these aircraft,

together with the development of the engine. Further, it was
agreed to set up a joint evaluation team that would enable
Britain, on behalf of NATO, to see if the aircraft was really
a winner or not. Here the Americans could not have been more
helpful; indeed, they have always continued to take an interest
in this project. But some of the frustrations that soon became
apparent are perhaps best indicated by the note which I was
obliged to send to the Chief Scientific Adviser to the Ministry
in November 1961, two years after I had started to try to foster
this particular piece of international collaboration:

> 'I am thoroughly dissatisfied with the way the P1127 is
> being handled. Whose fault this is I am not able to judge.
> But I now require an early and complete settlement of this
> project. If it is the Germans that are holding it up, I will
> immediately write to Strauss and tell him that he must
> settle now. If it is the Ministry of Aviation, then we must have
> an early meeting to which the Minister must come, and we
> must take firm decisions. If it is the Air Ministry who are
> trying still to hold back, then similar action must be taken
> with them. I hold no brief for or against this particular
> aircraft, but I think it is quite disgraceful that projects that
> come to Ministers and take up a good deal of time are then
> apparently allowed to fall back into inaction again.
> 'I should like an early report.'

It is with a wry sense of amusement that one must regard the
progress of this project over the next thirteen years. First the
Labour government cancelled what was to be the operational
aircraft, namely the P1154—the P1127 was never intended to
be more than a prototype. Then the government made a great
fuss about the breakthrough which the prototype represented
and reintroduced it under the name of the Harrier. It even
managed to sell some more to the United States, which had
always backed the concept. In the 1972 and 1973 White Papers
on Defence, the aircraft still appeared as one of the central

weapon systems of Britain's air defence. In 1974 it even moved
to the point, after all those years, where consideration was being
given to its use on naval ships as well as on land. In 1975 it
was again threatened with cancellation, but in the end the
maritime version was ordered. One can imagine what a company's shareholders would say about a project which appeared
in its annual reports for thirteen years without really advancing
beyond the original concept of the prototype.

The TSR2: An Expensive Change of Policy

The second case study underlines the almost unworkable
interface between industry and politics. It is the TSR2 project,
a 'tactical strategic reconnaissance' aircraft. When this
aircraft was cancelled I had left politics and was back in business,
but inadvertently I may have contributed to its demise, in a
note that I sent to the Chief of Defence Staff in May 1960:

> 'I am attracted by the idea that we could give the TSR2
> an increased strategic capacity by fitting it with some kind
> of missile. I understand that this is feasible, and I should be
> glad, therefore, if we could now examine this possibility in
> all our considerations of this aircraft. I hope that CSA can
> arrange for some talks with the firm, in order to find out a
> little more clearly what the possibilities are. These talks
> must, of course, be cleared with Aviation, but I hope they
> will be direct between the Ministry of Defence and Vickers.
>   'It seems to me that a very high cost aircraft like this
> must be given all the capacity that we can, and in any case
> I think there is a need in our plans for a low level launching
> vehicle for a missile.'

It was always just conceivable that the Americans might be
wrong in pinning the future of the deterrent to submarine-
based weapons like the Polaris and its successors. So, as the
British contribution to the strategic deterrent power of the
NATO alliance had inevitably to be limited, the TSR2 offered

some reinsurance, just in case the Russians found a complete answer to the Polaris submarine. The weapon I had in mind in my note was well within the capacity of the guidance control and power plant technology developed by English Electric for another first-class tactical nuclear weapon, 'Blue Water', which itself was not long to survive my departure from the Ministry of Defence. When the Labour government was looking for reasons to cancel the aircraft it is conceivable that its nuclear capacity may have been a factor.

To come back to the project itself: it was best described by *Flight Magazine* in October 1963:

> 'During the past decade, the persistent reluctance of the British Government to come to or maintain any decision regarding major programmes in the fields of aircraft, guided weapons or space, has resulted in a situation in which any all-British programme representing a really substantial advance on existing practice, is to be regarded as an exception and an achievement to be proud of.'

The TSR2 was an achievement of which the nation should have been very proud indeed. It was not an aircraft, but a total weapon system for which British industry had invented a wide range of secret equipment from advanced radars to micro-switches. With a wing span no bigger than a Spitfire's, the TSR2 was in itself a complete generation of advanced aircraft technology. Its flight envelope and performance specification was always ahead of the controversial American Swingwing aircraft, the F111, which the British government was unwise enough to believe would be a suitable substitute. I wrote in a letter to *The Times*, soon after Harold Wilson as Prime Minister had claimed that £250 million of public money would be saved if the TSR2 were cancelled and replaced by the F111:

> 'The Government says, and rightly, that the drive for more exports must have overall priority. It follows from this

that all the Government's own actions must seek to improve our export prospects.

'Yet its decisions, actual and potential, regarding the British aircraft industry are likely to do exactly the reverse. This industry has a very good export record. It must continue to make a major contribution to the future if we are to improve our overall export performance. If it is to make such a contribution, the industry must be able to spread its costs over a reasonable range of orders; it must not be subjected to continual changes of policy and lingering doubts about the future of important projects.

'It will be no solution to replace home production of military aircraft by purchases abroad on largely illusory arguments as to final cost. Such action would provide the worst of all possible solutions from an export point of view. One must hope that the Government really does understand that we can only be a successful export nation if our international image is that of an advanced technological society. Nothing does more damage in this regard than decisions to cancel British advanced technological projects in favour of purchases elsewhere.'

A great deal of Britain's reputation as an advanced technological nation went down the drain when this aircraft was cancelled. The first prototype model had flown and proved its capabilities, and the cost of the physical destruction of all its jigs and tools will never accurately be measured. Nor can the cost of frustrated design and production effort be estimated. The aircraft was not only a highly advanced and complicated weapon system; it also had the ability to take off from short and unpaved airstrips due to its unique undercarriage design. In addition, the aircraft pioneered a number of useful new management techniques; for example, it initiated split manufacturing arrangements, which worked well between Vickers and English Electric, and developed ministerial methods of monitoring the progress of the project, which led to new techniques of production management in government. Not all was lost, however, for much of the experience built into the Concorde was pioneered in the construction of the TSR2. Its short history highlights some of the management problems of inter-service rivalry as well as political misjudgement. The Navy opposed the project, its policy being to support the Buccaneer carrier-borne aircraft and to claim that this made the production of the TSR2 redundant. The Army did not like it much either, feeling that it was a highly expensive project which might affect the production of weapons like Blue Water, which it wanted for itself. The Royal Air Force, on the other hand, was quite certain that without the TSR2 the whole future of Britain's air power was in jeopardy. This led to some interesting discussions, first with the chiefs of staff and then in the Defence Committee, which of course is always chaired by the Prime Minister.

On 7 October 1960 I announced the placing of a full development contract involving the construction of nine TSR2 aircraft. I was only able to do that after putting my total ministerial and personal influence behind the project and making it plain to the Defence Committee that I stood or fell with it. It was in the end a management decision. Having weighed the evidence I made it. I am as sure that I was right as I am sure that the Labour government was tragically wrong in cancelling the project. In addition, I am certain that the Pentagon was equally wrong in refusing to share partly or wholly in the development or manufacture of the concept— an offer very generously made to them, in my presence, by Sir George Edwards in Washington. I think also, in the interests of NATO, that the Americans were wrong to seek to 'hard sell' the F111—to Harold Wilson as Prime Minister and Denis Healey as Minister of Defence—on the grounds that this aircraft would be as satisfactory as the TSR2 and far cheaper for Britain because Britain would be buying aircraft off the end of a long production run. In the end the nation paid more for cancelling the TSR2 and its American orders for the F111 than it would have cost it to build at least one squadron, and probably more, of TSR2s.

Supersonic Transport: Success at Last

Finally, the third case study provides some useful lessons about the desirability of developing advanced technology projects on a multinational basis. It is the project of the supersonic passenger jet mentioned in my minute to the Prime Minister in 1958 (already quoted on page 40). Clearly the Concorde project would never have been achieved had it not been a combined Anglo–French effort. Fortunately, each time one government lost its industrial and political nerve, the other was adamant. So Britain may yet achieve that 'blue riband' of the air that fate so rudely snatched away in the mid 1950s.

The project owes its inception and, I suspect, most of its survival to the ability of one man, namely Sir George Edwards. Twenty years ago the great issue in forward planning for air transport was where the barrier to the immediate upper limit of supersonic transport should lie. Should a supersonic transporter accept the limitations of the heat barrier at around Mach II? This would not involve the further immense risks of new structural technology. Below Mach II, aircraft can still be made of the conventional alloys and no fundamentally new technology or flight problems arise; above that speed, an all-steel or titanium aircraft and a new era of technology are involved. George Edwards always stuck to his view that the right thing to do was to go for the aircraft that, in his own words, 'Presented no really new problems.' Subsequent events have proved the rightness of his judgement and here, after so many years and so many other disappointments, is a project where Britain leads the Western world.

CONCLUSIONS

Many of the management conclusions from this case study chapter are self-evident. Two major considerations should be dealt with individually: the question of scale and the question of the relationship between political and industrial decision-making.

On the question of scale, it seems clear from the facts that competition on equal terms between the industries of the United Kingdom and of the United States is a practical impossibility because of the disparate scale of capacity and resources. The whole situation changes, however, when relative scale is considered in terms of the European Economic Community or even the most powerful industrial members of it. On this basis it should be possible to look American competition very straight in the eye. But for Britain alone the country must in future be more conscious of its industrial limitations.

Second, help in solving the problem of the relationship between political and industrial decision-making will come if it is recognised more clearly that real incompatibility does exist and that its degree rises with the complexity and scale of the decision. Every effort must be made to restrict direct government participation in industrial decision-making. Government should concentrate on 'holding the ring' for industrial activity, maintaining the value of money, preserving law and order and fulfilling the more classical view of its commitments. Governments today seem to find it hard enough to perform even these basic functions with success. The British economy may be a mixed one, but politics and business still do not mix well together. Many past mistakes would have been avoided if political decisions had not overriden those of management, and if governments had dealt more at arm's length with nationally and privately owned industry.

Chapter 4

NATIONALISATION
AND STATE CONTROL

A CASE OF FAILURE AT THE INTERFACE

In a study of the whole area of nationalisation and state control, it becomes obvious that the problems of persuading people to work together successfully have, in the context of British experience, been at their most acute in this sphere. This was to have been the sector of national life where direct ownership by the state was to motivate all concerned with a desire to serve the public interest. Certainly, if this inspirational approach had succeeded the nation would today be a great deal better off in almost every way. Instead, an essential sector of British industry has become a battleground of political ideology and human relationships to the inevitable detriment of technical progress. The battle still goes on unchecked.

The sincerity of the early socialist idealists who conceived the idea of national ownership cannot be challenged. Nor can it be denied that, after the immense stress of wartime operations, basic industries such as coal and the railways were in desperate need of rehabilitation. But, as so often happens, political ideology proved to be almost impossible to translate into workable management practice. After the socialist avalanche of 1945 the great nationalisation measures were fought through Parliament and, although the Conservative opposition pledged itself to at least a degree of denationalisation, the change was in fact largely irreversible. As he so often did, Winston Churchill summed up the correct national approach in his own inimitable way:

'We abhor the fallacy, for such it is, of nationalisation for nationalisation's sake. But where we are preserving it, as in the coal mines, the railways, air traffic, gas and electricity, we have done and are doing our utmost to make a success of it, even though this may somewhat mar the symmetry of party recrimination.'

Had the two main political parties accepted this as agreed doctrine, the nation would have been spared much pointless strife. But this was not to be.

The Railways

I will take the railways, as an example, at a period when I had personal knowledge of their problems. As Minister of Transport I inherited a transport policy which had grown out of the general election campaigns of 1950 and 1951, in which the Conservative Party had vigorously attacked nationalisation in all its forms. This had resulted in a statement of transport policy presented to Parliament in 1952 by the then Minister of Transport, which had announced the intention of the government to denationalise the road haulage side of the industry and to impose fairly wide management changes on British Railways under the heading of 'regionalisation and restructuring'. Meantime, the railway operating deficits were growing steadily and the total financial position of the railways was being undermined by falling freights and rising costs.

As always, the nub of the problem was to be found in the people involved. Businessmen serving on nationalised boards had left their parent ministries with no doubt of the bad effect on efficiency that was produced by politicians 'breathing down their necks'. But Conservative Members of Parliament supporting a Conservative government were increasingly and perhaps naturally pressing for better opportunities of breathing down nationalised necks and of demanding, if not complete denationalisation, then at least complete reorganisation. 'Rab' Butler played an important part here in co-ordinating policy; as always, he was calm, capable and immensely courteous. The trouble was to get time to take some sort of long calm look at the problem. I remember making a proposal to Rab Butler 'that we might have just an occasional Cabinet meeting, without officials, at which we could discuss some of these broad principles about nationalisation that meant so much to the future of our party and indeed to our country'. But somehow we never did have those meetings.

Meantime, the ritual dance between the government, the British Transport Commission and the railway trade unions continued. I had first seen this as Walter Monckton's Parliamentary Secretary, at the Ministry of Labour, when the country had faced the near certainty of a railway strike at the end of 1954. In the end this was averted, but only at the price of a very unhelpful statement by the court of inquiry, headed by Sir John Cameron, which said:

'We feel that we must state in the plainest of terms what we apprehend to be the proper approach. The nation has provided by statute that there shall be a nationalised system of railway transport, which must therefore be regarded as a public utility of the first importance. Having willed the "end", the nation must will the "means". This implies that employees of such a national service should receive a fair and adequate wage and that, in broad terms, the railwayman should be in no worse case than his colleagues in a comparable industry.'

The fundamental errors of the whole concept of national ownership could hardly have been set out more plainly. In the end the Prime Minister had to intervene. The Trades Union Congress was summoned to No. 10, and yet another compromise was patched up that in the end led to the appointment of the Guillebaud inquiry. All this political charade concealed the practical business facts of the case. These were that the British Transport Commission just could not afford to pay more wages without recovering them by increasing freight and passenger charges, a move which was politically unpopular and which, even worse, immediately drove more custom away from the railways.

Despite these continuing problems I felt very strongly that, as the responsible minister, I had to build a reasonable bridge of personal confidence between myself and Sir Brian Robertson, the then head of the British Transport Commission, and Sir John Elliott, head of London Transport. This was not too easy when ministerial contact under the hard pressure of events was often on a somewhat emotive level. I remember sitting facing Brian Robertson in the Carlton Club for something over thirty minutes, in complete silence, while he digested some of the disagreeable points that I had put to him as his minister. An even more difficult meeting was one held between Brian Robertson, John Elliott and myself in the Cavalry Club, where we rightly thought we should not be noticed, when the future of London Transport was under discussion. These odd meetings were necessary because formal consultation between the Minister of Transport and the Chairman of the British Transport Commission or of London Transport were almost entirely inhibited by the rules that Parliament had laid down. The chairmen were totally responsible for the day-to-day conduct of their affairs. The Minister held only the responsibilities of representing the public interest, if he knew where it lay, and of defending the commission in Parliament. This situation had been interpreted by Lord Hurcomb, the first Chairman of the British Transport Commission, as one leading to a relationship of total non-cooperation between the commission and the Ministry. As a previous Permanent Secretary of the Ministry of Transport he had certainly known how to implement such a policy. So the dialogue was a difficult one, for in a less political world Lord Hurcomb would have been right. Yet in spite of these difficulties, I was very conscious that Brian Robertson, on his part, was rightly trying to build up links of personal confidence between himself and his colleagues on the commission, and the railwaymen and the railways' customers.

Slowly the great modernisation plan for the railways was

grinding on, and here at least some of the decisions were being taken that bear fruit today. Some £1,500 million was already committed, although too much of it had to be allocated to overtake arrears of maintenance arising from the inevitable neglect of the war years. These arrears had been allowed to run on into the postwar period because arguments about nationalisation had replaced action to make the railways efficient and viable. In spite of this, the replacement of steam locomotives by diesel and electric traction was going ahead. The long welded rail had been introduced. Hundreds of miles of track were being resignalled and fitted with automatic train controls, and major electrification schemes were being pressed forward, particularly on the London–Midland route from Euston to Manchester and Liverpool and eventually to Scotland. All this, it was realised, was essential for the future existence of the railways, as were new concepts of passenger comfort and freight transport. Brian Robertson's experience in the Control Commission in West Germany after the war fitted him well to head this sort of operation. The problem was to keep the impetus going and to close enough inefficient branch lines, so that viability might eventually be attained. The urgent policy discussions between the Chairman of the British Transport Commission and myself, as Minister of Transport and Civil Aviation, in the autumn of 1958, were as good an example as any of the kind of difficulties a minister and his chairman constantly faced. The railways had come forward to say that, due to a grave fall in bulk and heavy traffics, their deficit was rising at an alarming rate. Much of this derived from the famous 'plan for the nationalised coal industry' on which the railways had based much of their forward estimates of freight traffic. The plan had totally over-estimated both the production and the consumption of coal, with consequent severely adverse effects on the railways' future planning. As a result of these discussions the government had to publish a White Paper which concluded:

'The finances of British Railways have been struck a

violent, unexpected blow by the sharp setback in the output and traffics of coal, steel and other basic industries.

'Having no reserves to meet such an emergency, temporary though it may be, the Commission are facing a financial crisis of gravity and urgency. The question is—what should be done about it?'

As always, the Ministry of Transport, together with the British Transport Commission, tried to take a more hopeful look at the future. There would have to be a further reduction in costs, and further efforts would be needed to increase revenue, which meant increasing fares and charges. In return for what were largely unstructured forecasts, I was authorised by the Cabinet to add a further £25 million to the accumulated deficit of the railways and to accept as justification the promise of further savings in working costs and the expedition of parts of the management plan. And so the process continued: consultation, conciliation and disappointed hopes. It was no single person's fault—certainly not the fault of Sir Brian Robertson or his colleagues in management. Parliament, in its wisdom, had decreed that the railways should be nationalised. Much time had been lost in the arid political discussions that followed and in the long debates in Parliament and in the country on nationalisation. These debates only clouded the practical issues at a time when the best intellects available should have been bending their total skill and energy towards trying to make a success of an industry that was dying—or, at least, rapidly declining so far as its place in the economy was concerned.

Now the country was reaping the inevitable consequences of putting politics before management. These strains obviously exerted their maximum disruptive force at the interface of personal contact: (a) between the Minister of Transport and the Conservative Party both in and out of the House of Commons, and (b) between the Minister and those chairmen of nationalised industry for whom he was responsible. Under these conditions, I think it is surprising that it was possible to establish any reasonable relationships at all. It was greatly to Sir Brian Robertson's credit that he, in his turn, managed to carry his British Transport Commission colleagues with him and, despite the difficulties, began to attract the loyalty and support of the railwaymen. So some progress was made and more could have been achieved if it had been possible to build on the relationships which had been slowly and painfully built up over the three years in which Brian Robertson and I, as his minister, tried to do our best with an intractable situation. Brian Robertson had begun to attract the confidence of the working railwaymen, as a fair and impartial head of the commission. The movement now was towards a policy of continuity in the modernisation plan in which lay the only hope for a practical business future for the railways and thus for the railwaymen. It is a fundamental criticism of the whole concept of nationalisation to have to record that this continuity of management—perhaps the most essential requirement for a successful railway system—proved, in the event, to be unattainable. This was not only because radical changes of policy were made when a government changed, but also because within each main political party there was rethinking going on about nationalisation which translated itself into a continued demand to pull up the growing plant in order to examine its roots.

For example, it was probably too much to ask politically of my successor as Minister of Transport that, instead of replacing Brian Robertson, the government should have found a first-class managing director for him and so have got the best of both worlds. The continuing enforced changes of policy under Lord Beeching and his successors, against the *leit motif* of continuing industrial strife and worsening service, underline my own experience in this field.

AN UNEASY PARTNERSHIP

This uneasy relationship remains inevitable so long as a degree of direct political control can be exercised in Britain's basic industries. The nationalisation statutes may lay down that ministers should not interfere in day-to-day policy, but so long as the prices of coal, steel, electricity, gas and railway tickets remain a political issue the temptation to interfere by one means or another is overwhelming. In practice, all governments have used the nationalised industries as instruments of policy; this has been particularly so with price or wage restraint, for example. This interference has often frustrated technical progress and damaged personal relationships at all levels. Yet, for an understanding of the total problem, full account has to be taken of the pressures on a minister who is responsible, if not directly accountable, for nationalised industry. So the lesson remains. If nationalised industry is to be effectively managed, it has to be free of ministerial interference and operated by managers who adhere to the basic principles of free enterprise.

STATE CONTROL AND THE MINISTERIAL ROLE

Britain's roads were built by private enterprise, but their planning, development and programme control rested with ministers. As a result the road programme was often impeded by purely political considerations. First let me give an example of the kind of political row that can blow up in the House of Commons, where a minister is thought to be vulnerable to attack for his policies. The Preston bypass, although a comparatively minor scheme, was in the late 1950s one of Britain's first essays in motor road building. That it existed at all at that time was very much a tribute to the drive and efficiency of a remarkable man, James Drake, who was Chief Engineer and Bridgemaster of Lancashire County Council. I felt at that time that his drive and enterprise in getting this piece of motor road constructed against immense difficulties should be rewarded by as much publicity as I could get for him as an encouragement to other local authorities. So I persuaded Harold Macmillan, as Prime Minister, to open the road in December 1958. I had

had some anxieties about its construction in one of the wettest parts of England where, of necessity, over $3\frac{1}{2}$ million tons of earth had been excavated and nearly 1 million tons of imported filling material had been brought in to strengthen the many embankments. Filling material included red shale, which at that time was an unused road-building material. The Ministry of Transport described this road as a 'guinea pig'; in other words, it was an experiment for all other British motorways. I had been anxious to look at its progress for myself, but my visit during the construction stage was frustrated by the fact that the Ministry's aircraft, a de Havilland Dove, in which I was travelling, 'lost' one engine halfway to Lancashire and had to return to London Airport. I was not unduly surprised to be told about a month after the opening that there was a limited amount of 'frost heave' which had affected about 1 or 2 per cent of the carriageway surface. Frost heave is caused by excessive moisture just below the road surface which, on freezing, causes ripples in the top surface layer. Under heavy traffic conditions the road surface thus affected can break up into pot holes if the problem is not dealt with quickly. Because much of the road was on high embankments, which at that time were not fully guarded, the Ministry's advice was to close the road totally for repair less than two months after it had been opened. In fact, repairs might have been managed without total closure, but this seemed the safest and quickest way of putting matters right.

Because I was involved in intricate negotiations with the British Transport Commission on legislation, I was perhaps a little slow to realise the magnitude of the row that this would cause and to realise how soon those who had been criticising the Ministry for not building roads fast enough would happily turn to criticising it for not knowing how to build roads anyway. My own personal position as a minister was soon under heavy attack in both the press and the House of Commons. Anyone would have thought that I had designed and built the road myself! The Prime Minister asked me if I was worried by the attacks and I said no in what I hoped was a reasonably confident tone, but I knew my personal position as Minister was precarious in the extreme if I did not beat off the attack. I decided, therefore, that the right thing to do was to support the road-building authority, namely the Lancashire County Council and James Drake's department in particular. It was fortunate for me that the Lancashire County Council at that time had a Labour majority. This made it difficult for the opposition to attack me without attacking its own local authority, which I was stoutly defending. So after a fairly abrasive few days, when I could hardly bear to open a newspaper, much less lift the telephone, that particular problem was behind the Ministry.

This period also provides a good example of the pressures which are part of ministerial life but which rarely present themselves to managers in industry. In the middle of the Preston crisis, just as I was being told by an eminent civil engineer that the total road design was basically faulty (a view which fortunately proved to be incorrect), my Private Secretary (Air) burst into my office to say that a Viscount aircraft bringing the Turkish Prime Minister on an official visit to Britain had crashed at Gatwick and that all the occupants of the aircraft were dead. This statement was also happily incorrect, but ministerial life at this time was certainly full of a number of excitements on road, rail and air, to say nothing of a few rows in shipping. Even at home my telephone rang in the early hours with the fateful words, 'Minister, I think you ought to know . . .'. Few businessmen expect to be woken at two or three o'clock in the morning by tales of disaster or, even worse, by a pressman who invites you to reply to a press comment in the first edition of a newspaper that you have not even read. Politics has methods of putting the pressure on ministers that are beyond the wildest dreams of shareholders or even shareholder committees.

Part of my task as Minister of Transport obviously was to try to encourage the private enterprise contractors and their men to press forward with what was often a very difficult and even risky job. For example, in building the first section of the

M1 motorway between London and Birmingham, John Laing and Company faced a major challenge. On starting the work on 24 March 1958 I said with truth: 'I am starting work on the largest single road scheme ever commissioned in this country.' The statistics were daunting:

Nearly 70 miles of road to build at a rate of 1 mile every 10 days;
12 million cubic yards or 16 million tons of muck to shift— 'muck' being the right term for much of it;
134 bridges to build at a rate of $1\frac{1}{2}$ bridges per week;
80,000 horsepower deployed in plant and equipment.

The Ministry had wagered £16 million of its scarce road money on the project. If the project failed, all the Ministry's road plans would be set back and the chances of its getting any more money would be much diminished. But I had great confidence in the splendid team of men in the Ministry, in the civil engineers and in the contractors. I believed that if it were humanly possible to do it, then it would be done, and in the end so it was, just after I had left the Ministry. It was immensely to the credit of three men in particular—Maurice Laing, John Mitchell, his project engineer, and Sir Owen Williams, the consulting civil engineer—that success was achieved.

I tried to visit as many road schemes as possible. On my way to open the Stamford bypass—an important section of the rebuilt A1 road system—I was asked, on the roadside by BBC television, to comment off the cuff on a recently published report of a House of Commons Estimates Select Committee on the cost and thus the progress of the road programme. Such committees are 'of the whole House'; in other words, they are comprised of all political parties and they report 'to the House' as a whole, often with much publicity. They can, and do, take evidence from a minister's civil servants and from outside experts, but they normally do not take evidence from the minister himself. The press held that this committee had severely criticised the whole road programme and, by implication, the local authorities and civil engineering firms which were now grappling with the task of getting it forward. In an endeavour to defend those who were building the roads against those who were merely criticising them, I used some sharp words. These were held to have criticised not only the report submitted to Parliament by the Estimates Committee, but also the committee itself—a matter which, in the view of at least some members of the opposition who served on the committee, demanded a formal apology to Parliament. This, on the whole, I was unwilling to give, because I felt that what I had said in defence of those who were getting on with the job was justifiable. I preferred to rest on the detailed answer which the Ministry would have to present to the select committee as soon as this could be prepared. I felt very strongly at this time that the whole road programme might be prejudiced if those struggling with the difficulties felt that they could be taken to task by Parliament the first time that some detailed aspect of the programme went wrong. After all, the Estimates Committee had said that the programme was inadequately prepared and was out of proportion, which I felt was unfair. Fortunately, at this time I got a good deal of support from the press and the maximum understanding from the then chairman of the select committee. But the House rose with the issue still unresolved and certainly with some members of the Estimates Committee thirsting for my blood.

In retrospect, ministerial office sometimes strikes a lighter note. Almost my first ministerial act, as Minister of Transport, was to promise Sir Herbert Manzoni and the Birmingham City Council £100,000 to start the Birmingham Inner Ring Road. I was visiting the city as a newly appointed minister. I knew it well as an ex-businessman and I had always felt that the city fathers ought to do something about the Bull Ring. Here was a chance, it seemed, to apply a bit of help to what looked like a very businesslike scheme. As I did it without departmental or Treasury authority, this was where, as a businessman, I learned my first ministerial lesson.

Later, almost at the end of my ministerial term in the Ministry of Transport, I was asked to finish ceremoniously the demolition work on the same scheme. The plan was to blow up a wall containing the last bricks of the old Bull Ring. The charge was tamped too well. The boom was very satisfying— urban explosions were still a novelty in those days—but the effect was alarming. The wall disintegrated and went up into the air in a mushroom cloud of dust and much more solid objects. Amid a hail of brickbats from the sky, the Minister and civic dignitaries fled for their lives.

Brickbats and bouquets, ministers get them both, but mainly brickbats. These are delivered in a way which is totally strange to anything the normal manager in business experiences. Cross-questioning in the House of Commons far outstrips the roughest shareholders' meeting. Select committees look like a Star Chamber compared with managements' experience of interrogation. Few businessmen would welcome a situation where they had to face their shareholders at least once a week in a debate where, subject only to the Speaker as chairman, no holds were barred.

The moral for management to draw is that in the British 'mixed' economy there are many incompatible ingredients. A minister's responsibilities to his department, to Parliament and to the electorate are worlds apart from the present accountability of managers and management. So it is not surprising that, whether it be in the sphere of national policy or of relationships with nationalised industry, there can be wide areas of mutual mistrust and misunderstanding. This situation, it must be reiterated, is unlikely to improve unless government pulls back as far as possible from detailed involvement in industrial management on the part of ministers.

As far as existing nationalised industry is concerned, the advice of the Confederation of British Industry is clear: management must be allowed to manage under the direction of boards and chairmen who are not subject to the detailed

political pressures of the past. This advice has been repeatedly
supported by the chairmen of nationalised industry themselves.
The fact that the proposed method of nationalising the shipbuilding and aerospace industries is somewhat different does
not alter this requirement. It is to be hoped that these industries
will not become political shuttlecocks. Pledges to denationalise
would simply be met with a promise to renationalise, a process
which would make good industrial management totally
impossible. Where the control of government is exercised
through its shareholding, as in Rolls-Royce or British Leyland,
then a new situation for management is faced. Here the
Conservative Industries Act of 1972 at least laid down that
such shareholdings must be disposed of by government as soon
as possible. The National Enterprise Board seems likely to
take a more possessive view of company shareholdings. If so,
events will prove such a management theory to be no more
practical than other forms of direct state control. It could also
lead to the same continuing controversy over interventionist
agencies such as NEB, as there is over nationalisation, with
corresponding damage to good management practice.

A more hopeful and practical trend is to be seen in the
creation, by the Bank of England and other City institutions, of
'finance for industry' as a term lender of last resort. There is,
in the City of London, a new and more vigorous determination
for the City to preserve its historic role as a provider of capital
resources for industry. This must surely be the right alternative
to state shareholding and takeovers and all managers, although
they may not fully understand City mystique, should welcome
such developments as a viable and workable alternative to state
share purchase. Somehow, to quote Winston Churchill again,
'the symmetry of party recrimination' must be marred in this
vital sector of British industry. If practical experience is to be the
guide for the future, then it must be more clearly realised that
the state operates under parliamentary rules that will always
make it a clumsy and inefficient entrepreneur.

Chapter 5

PEOPLE AT WORK

Ultimately our world is about people, not about things. So it is in the context of people at work that any attempt to sum up the failures and missed opportunities of the postwar period has to be made. Over this span, equal to much of a man's working life, there has been no lack of good advice; nor has there been any lack of leaders among politicians, trade unionists and industrialists, who have been prepared to promote the concept of a nation of people working together as a team for agreed objectives. If the reasons why the results have been disappointing, on the whole, could be clearly defined, then a knowledge of what has to be done to achieve success in the future would be much nearer. Seeking guidance from past history, it might perhaps be said that, if two leaders in this field, Walter Monckton and Godfrey Ince (at the head of the then Ministry of Labour), had received more support from Winston Churchill in the immediate postwar period, success could have been achieved. The chances of success were greater at that time than they have ever been since. Trade union leadership was stronger and personal relationships were closer over a wide spread of industry and government than they are today. So it is worth starting the analysis in those early postwar years when some of the team spirit of the comradeship of war still lingered on.

A NEW APPROACH

Before I was appointed by Sir Winston Churchill to be Walter Monckton's junior minister, I had written in 1950, with Ted

Leather and four of my other back bench colleagues, a pamphlet on industrial relations entitled 'A New Approach'. It had been well received by the press and its main theme was partnership. We wrote then—and twenty-five years after it is still true:

'*Partnership the Solution*

'Our conception of the new industrial pattern and the solution of the productivity problem is a human one.

'It is "partnership", the free and equal partnership of the individual elements of the State, the Trade Unions and the Employers, working together for the good of all.

'In this partnership the first duty of the State is to ensure that hard and efficient work, at any level in the industrial scale, gets its fair reward, unadulterated by excessive taxes or restrictive practices.

'The country desperately needs a high output, high earnings policy, founded on the belief that the more money a man earns, for which he has honestly worked, the better for him and for society as a whole. The State, by better national housekeeping, must make it possible for the worker to retain a larger proportion of his earnings, to be spent as he pleases, not as the State directs.

'The Government must consult industry and organised labour at a much earlier stage during the formulation of its economic policy. Bodies such as the National Production Advisory Council on Industry and the Regional Boards for Industry, on which Employers and the Unions are fully represented, must be used to a much greater extent and their advice fully considered.'

I found that these views were not out of line with what Walter Monckton was trying to achieve as Minister of Labour. Later Lord Monckton, he was a powerful figure in Winston Churchill's Cabinet and was respected by both parties in the Commons. His distinguished legal background made the ideal non-partisan base for an acceptable approach to both employers and trade unionists. First he had been supported by a junior minister in the person of Peter Bennett (later Lord Bennett, head of the Lucas Company). When Peter Bennett found the strain of long days and nights in the House too much, Winston Churchill asked me to succeed him.

AN ESSAY IN PARTNERSHIP

The Ministry of Labour, with the strong backing of the Prime Minister, was launched on an essay in partnership in industry. For a time this project seemed to prosper. Relationships between the Minister of Labour and leaders of the trade union movement, such as Arthur Deakin of the Transport and General Workers' Union, were on a practical and friendly basis. Walter Monckton asked me to look after some areas of this unofficial, but not unimportant, liaison. So it was at this stage that I found myself working very closely with Victor Feather (now Lord Feather) who was an Assistant General Secretary of the Trades Union Congress at that time. This relationship was put to a fairly severe test by the London dock strike in the autumn of 1954. Behind the strike was considerable friction between the rival unions of the National Amalgamated Stevedores and Dockers and the Transport and General Workers' Union. As I said in a speech at the time, 'It is bad human relations leading to a complete lack of knowledge of the true facts of the case on the part of the vast majority of the men.' A bitter phrase in the Ministry of Labour at that time was that relations in the docks were so bad that if you hired a man on a bicycle to ride round the docks shouting, 'Everybody out', you would have a strike on your hands. It was a measure of the satisfactory level of co-operation that Walter Monckton had achieved that the General Purposes Committee of the TUC issued a statement which 'deplored action likely to destroy effective relationships in industry and the established machine of collective bargaining', and which further added 'the General Council of the TUC could see no purpose in continuing what is a useless sacrifice which could achieve nothing and must finally be disposed of by a normal process of collective bargaining'.

At this time, the Ministry was labouring away at what was sometimes called the 'Ince plan'. This was an attempt to establish a model constitution which would result in an automatic arbitration procedure in all industries, the long-term objective being to make strikes unnecessary and outmoded. Where this enterprise failed was in the belief that it could all be done by moral persuasion and that agreement to voluntary arbitration as a final settlement of disputes could be achieved in every major industry. If the plan had succeeded, it would in the end have made lockouts and strikes unnecessary. Perhaps this was the moment at which the government should have legislated to bring this about. The strongest man in the trade union movement at this time was Arthur Deakin, who retained much of the bluff common sense and practical approach to industrial problems of his predecessor, Ernest Bevin. He was to be one of the last of the trade union leaders who could deliver a bargain, personally made by himself, and override the militants in his union. Together with Tom Williamson of the Municipal and General Workers' Union, Bill Carron of the Amalgamated Union of Engineering Workers, and others, he formed part of a generation of strong men at the head of the largest unions. Thus the situation for progress, had it been possible to see it, was as favourable as would ever be achieved in the postwar years. Relations on the Ministry of Labour's consultative mini-parliament were also very good at this time. The National Joint Advisory Council, which met at the Ministry, covered all sides of industry effectively and provided a forum where industrial problems could be discussed in a calm and factual way.

I was very anxious that this body should take a stand on the whole subject of human relations in industry and it was on my own initiative that the Ministry published a document on 'Human Relations in Industry', trying to pull together some threads of this whole complex subject. The basic recommendation was that new steps should be taken to try to bring together employers and workpeople to face the hard facts of the economic and trading position of Britain. It placed quite squarely on employers the responsibility for achieving good relations on the shopfloor and encouraged them to try to set the wider responsibility for telling their workpeople fully and frankly about the fortunes of the enterprise in which they worked. At this time too neither the British Employers' Confederation nor the TUC was looking for any kind of industrial showdown, so most factors were in the Ministry's favour. Perhaps this was the nearest point that was reached to the goal of a new approach.

The situation in the House of Commons too was as favourable as it could have been, with Alf Robens, later Lord Robens, as Shadow Minister of Labour—a man who was prepared to do his best to carry his party with him on a policy of reasonable conciliation. Nor were relationships between the TUC and the Prime Minister unfriendly at this time. I remember a clear example of this in the Thompson dispute. Mr Thompson was a tough newspaper proprietor of the old school who owned, among other things, the *Dundee Courier and Advertiser*. He was not a believer in any kind of relationship with trade unions. In fact, his employees were required to sign an undertaking not to join a union. It was clear that this relatively minor dispute was likely to be elevated by the trade union movement to a matter of major principle. It did, after all, involve the right of an employee to join a trade union. Winston Churchill, in the absence of Walter Monckton who was ill, obviously felt that he should agree to a request from the TUC to see him and thus should move in and seek to defuse the situation. So leading members of the TUC's General Council were summoned to No. 10 in September 1952. There, with some ceremony, they were seated round the cabinet table and presented with large glasses of whisky, while they were regaled by the Prime Minister with a general discussion of broad affairs of state. Meantime, I was shuttling backwards and forwards between the cabinet room and a telephone line to Mr Thompson's office, seeking to get his final agreement to a form of words discussed with the Ministry which would end the firm's insistence on an agreement not to belong to any trade union. This proved a somewhat difficult operation, with the man at the other end not particularly willing to collaborate. Each time I returned to the Prime Minister with the latest state of play, I looked to see a worsening of the atmosphere between him and the congress members. But this presented no difficulty to Winston Churchill and, towards the end, the trade union leaders were very willingly being instructed by the Prime Minister in the theory and practice of running racehorses as a method of tax loss.

With this prevailing mood for a short period it looked as if success might be grasped with a new concept of industrial relations. However, the attempt failed because (with the benefit of hindsight) the efforts being made were clearly not pressed home hard enough. The Prime Minister harked back to his wartime leadership and believed that the battle to rebuild economic Britain would achieve the same unity, given his leadership, as the Battle of Britain itself. All the Ministry of Labour's training as a great advocate led him to plead his cause rather than to force it on all concerned. The trade unions too were fumbling towards a new role in postwar Britain, never better illustrated than by the galumphing great carthorse by which cartoonist Low always represented the TUC. They too were not seeking any activist role. The Conservative Party in opposition had produced a blueprint of its own, 'The Industrial Charter'; but Rab Butler, who was very much in charge of Conservative thought and policy, did not seek at the time to translate this into a precise legislative programme. Now it all seems a long time ago. Yet, because the mythology of the industrial events of the 1930s—the miners, the Jarrow marchers, and all the rest—still conditions to some extent the industrial relations of the 1970s, the whole of this postwar period too must be examined if an understanding is to be gained of what chances were really missed and what could now be done about it in the second half of this century.

THE CHANCE IS MISSED

So the years with Walter Monckton slipped by, years in which I learned much of tolerance and patience and made friendships in the trade union movement that have survived. I don't think any government since the war has been nearer to a practical working partnership between the three estates of the realm: organised labour, organised employers and the government. Had Winston Churchill been five years younger, had Walter Monckton not had to expend so much of his precious energy on the enervating processes of endless conciliation, a spark might have been struck that would have fired subsequent industrial history. Walter Monckton was a great Minister of Labour and did more for his country and the Conservative Party than most people are prepared to recognise. Looking back, I feel certain that the prize of partnership was then nearer to being grasped than it has been since.

Winston Churchill resigned and Sir Anthony Eden took his place. Now the industrial sky was darkening fast with the threat of a rail strike, based on worsening relationships between the British Transport Commission and the three rail unions, hanging over the Ministry. By the time Anthony Eden had formed his government, the Ministry was in rough industrial waters again. Had the circumstances been more favourable, Anthony Eden as Prime Minister would, I believe, have taken a much more activist view of the concept of partnership in industrial relations. My next visit to Chequers was at an informal and private discussion between the new Prime Minister and some trade union leaders. Then an important meeting was held at No. 10 in November 1955 between the Prime Minister, the Chancellor of the Exchequer, Walter Monckton, myself and a strong trade union delegation representing the TUC's General Council and containing powerful figures like Tom Williamson, Harry Douglas and Lewis Wright, together with Vincent Tewson and George Woodcock. The purpose of the meeting was to see whether we could come to any agreement about a wages and prices policy; but the TUC hedged all their bets. They said that they had no authority to interfere in wage settlements. They had done their best to seek restraint, but many of their members expected them to attack a Conservative government and this made the situation very difficult for them. The General Council could not issue a general statement calling for restraint since it could not be applicable to all unions. The rise in purchase tax was the main cause of discontent. Rab Butler handled the meeting well, but I felt there was no great meeting of minds, although still a great deal of goodwill on the surface. Probably by then the psychological moment had passed. It is interesting to speculate what would have happened to a legislative prices policy, coupled with a provision for the automatic arbitration of disputes, if the government had brought it in at that time. It might just have succeeded.

When I left the Ministry of Labour for the Ministry of Transport, I left a note on relations with the trade union movement for my successor, Robert Carr. In it I said:

'Our long term objective should surely remain that of bringing the Trade Union Movement towards the central position in the State divorced from close affinity with any political party. We are most likely to encourage this developing tendency towards middle of the roadism, if we continue to involve the TUC as much as possible in Government policy and to work closely with it at all times. Because for four years we have created much confidence and trust, it is easy to forget how quickly all this can be swept away.'

And swept away it was in the tide of Suez and the political free-for-all that followed. Yet at least these years were an attempt at a new approach that still has a relevant lesson today. Although it did not succeed in its main aim, at least it provided a basis on which future Ministers of Labour were able to have a continuing dialogue with the trade union movement.

A CONTINUING ATTEMPT AT UNITY

However circumstances may change, some sort of dialogue must continue between successive governments, the trade unions and the employers. There have been many variations on the theme of unity. The continuing purpose of Conservative governments and the employers' organisations has, on the whole, been to try to persuade the trade union movement to take a more independent stance. On the other hand, if only for reasons of financial support, Labour governments have sought to involve the unions even more closely in the structure of the Labour Party.

Certain major initiatives in this latter part of the postwar period must be noted. First among these is the foundation of the National Economic Development Council. A Britain plagued with a continuing imbalance between its unit costs and those of its competitors has been forced into many devices to try to keep a reasonable balance between wages and prices. The Stafford Cripps' wage freeze was the only successful attempt at this form of control, until the dam broke, because the government at that time still wielded all the apparatus of rationing and wartime controls. The 'three wise men' and the 'guiding light' were Conservative initiatives followed by the NEDC concept put forward by Selwyn Lloyd as Chancellor of the Exchequer. This piece of machinery has survived; it will be the subject of study in Chapters 6 and 8.

Second must be noted the attempt by the succeeding Labour government to introduce statutory wage controls. The government's White Paper entitled 'In Place of Strife' was, in the circumstances of the time, a bold and constructive attempt to impose a long-term policy of wage restraint. However, the details of the policy were not as interesting as the reaction of the trade union movement. The TUC rapidly adopted an attitude of complete opposition to the whole concept. The important fact, in the light of subsequent events, was that after prolonged negotiations the White Paper was withdrawn and replaced by a 'compact' on wage restraint between the TUC and the Labour government. Even this required the intervention of Harold Wilson as Prime Minister. In other words, in the view of many trade unionists, the TUC had prevailed against the government of the day.

A CHANGE FOR THE WORSE

Here was the beginning of a long wrangle between the TUC and successive governments. This confrontation steadily eroded the fundamental principle on which industrial relations had previously been based: the principle that in the end a democratically elected government must always prevail against any sectional interest in the state, however powerful. One cannot but recall Sir Godfrey Ince's reiterated advice to Walter Monckton: 'Minister, if you fight a battle with the unions, you must win and be seen to win' Surprisingly enough, the Conservative government appeared to take little heed of its predecessor's defeat and introduced its own plan for the reorganisation of industrial relations. When drafted as an election document, 'People at Work', this might well have made a useful contribution. Once it was drafted in legal form as a bill by the government's lawyers, it contained a great number of potentially dangerous industrial trip-wires. Strong representations were made to the government about the dangers inherent in legal sanctions which would involve trade unionists going to prison, but the bill went forward in all its legal panoply. As a result the trade unions once again declared war on a government measure and, although this time it took a general election to achieve their ends, again in their own eyes they could claim to have succeeded against the government. They had secured the abandonment of a major piece of government policy by the repeal of the Industrial Relations Act 1970. Now many left wing trade unionists felt that they had defeated both political parties. The Communists, Maoists and Trotskyists rejoiced.

Against this background a much more enlightened initiative was to be heavily handicapped. No Prime Minister has ever devoted as much care and patience as Edward Heath did to seeking to bring about tripartite agreement between the Confederation of British Industry, the TUC and the Government on the cure for Britain's economic ills. Had the Industrial Relations Act not soured relationships, the initiative might well have succeeded. Indeed, under the pressure of the miners' strike of 1973 and the consequent 'three-day week' in industry, the CBI and the TUC were very close to an agreement that could have got the government off the hook of its statutory Phase 3 wages policy as applied to the miners. But once again, under the hard abrasive pressure of day-to-day events, the chance was missed and the Prime Minister decided to put the issue to the electorate. By then the issue was confused. The detailed arguments are no concern of this study; what matters to the future course of industrial events is that, after the general election and a Labour victory, the miners were given their full pay demands by the new government and within a year were to succeed again with a pay claim which was well in excess of the voluntary wage contract which the government had agreed with the TUC. All this apparent success for the application of crude industrial power and militancy by sectional interest is a new factor in British public life. Small wonder that the left wing claims a victory over capitalism and that much of the current Labour Party policy is based on a necessity to agree with the unions and their activist left wing, to the virtual exclusion of other interests.

Looking back at thirty years of people at work in this postwar period, I see a constant attempt by men of goodwill of all political persuasions, by politicians, employers and trade union leaders, to achieve mutual agreement. So far the nation has been denied the great gain in industrial efficiency and social well-being that would follow from such an agreement. Many people would now say that the concept of working together is further away than ever. Others point to growing left wing and Communist strength, as they see it, and to the end of capitalism and free enterprise as Britain has known it.

The situation is neither as depressing nor as hopeful as the right and left wings respectively see it. After two major failures by Labour and Conservative governments to get agreement on legislative backing for wage control or trade union reform, much has clearly been lost. In this field, at least, organised protest and militancy has paid off and it is as well that the Labour Party, which encouraged this militant attitude, has had to cope with its implications. But matters will not stay as they are. Growing opposition by people to control from the top will provide a new opportunity to those who are willing to build up with patience and perseverance from the bottom. In the next phase it is what happens at the shopfloor and plant levels that will be significant. Here is a unique chance to build a more durable form of industrial democracy based on participation at the shopfloor, plant and company levels.

Meantime, events at the national level are now not entirely under British control. As a continuing member of the European Economic Community, in the long term Britain is unable to conduct its industrial relations in isolation. If the country cannot agree its own preferred solution, it will be forced to conform to a continental pattern of industrial relationship, which is not in any way designed to take account of British requirements or practice. Once again in this sphere, as in others, great opportunities have been lost in the postwar era. Yet the long and bumpy road from Tolpuddle has not yet reached a dead end. The steady devolution of power downwards in the British social and industrial system provides a new opportunity to attain the goal of unity of purpose and action. Rising unemployment and harder times in 1975 may be the catalyst that will ensure basic reconsideration of our present pattern of industrial relationships.

THE EMPLOYERS' SIDE OF THE PICTURE

While most of the action has taken place on the industrial
relations front, with the government and the TUC as the main
protagonists, it would be wrong to ignore significant developments on the employers' side of the picture. The old British Employers' Federation has gone, as has some of the power of the
chambers of trade and commerce. It was inevitable that the unitary approach of organised labour under the TUC should breed
a similar development among employers. Hence, the Confederation of British Industry is now regarded by successive governments, together with the TUC, as the relevant negotiating
instrument. The comparative positions of these two bodies need
understanding. The TUC is often accorded a more powerful
voice than it deserves. In fact it has little power over its constituent members and it does not even represent a majority
of all employees. The CBI, on the other hand, often gets credit
for less influence than it could have, and in some cases does
have, over employers. It is the only body that over recent years
has persuaded its members to adopt an effective voluntary
price freeze, at least for a period. It is the only body that
provides representation on its committees and on its Grand
Council to almost all trade associations, to most British companies large and small, to the City and to the professions, such
as accountancy and banking.

Yet the suspicion exists that, when Edward Heath sought to
construct an economic policy based on advice given to the
government by the CBI and TUC, he and his officials found
neither of these bodies able to deliver what the Whitehall
machine required. The TUC was better at the dialectic, but in
the end it wielded only the negative power of disruption. The
CBI had not, by the nature of its constitution as a confederation,
the ability to deliver a clear and succinct economic policy
translatable into political terms without continuing an often
difficult consultation with its membership. After all, the CBI
stood for free enterprise and the market economy, in which

the entrepreneur was king. When, by a considerable act of leadership from Sir John Partridge, the then President, and Campbell Adamson, the Director General, the confederation persuaded its membership to offer a policy of voluntary price restraint to the government, it was bitterly disappointed at the results. The TUC did not respond with any attempt at voluntary wage restraint on its part, and the government's subsequent actions on legislative controls looked to many CBI members like a smack in the face for the confederation. Since then the CBI has done a great deal to rethink its philosophy and to realign it with changed circumstances. Through the work of powerful committees of businessmen on economic policy, employment policy, company affairs and Europe, to name only a few areas, it has begun to hammer out the kind of clear united policy that it must have if it is to play a significant role in reshaping Britain's affairs.

The CBI, like the TUC, will have to re-examine its power base. At the moment neither body has effective control over its membership, to the extent that it can undertake to 'deliver' a policy by ensuring that all its members will implement it. The TUC is, of course, a much more politically motivated body than the CBI. But the Confederation is now seeing the necessity of acting more to influence events and policy in advance and of taking a more political line where this is necessary. In 'Industry and Government', a report produced by a small high-level steering group of industrialists and published in July 1974, the CBI made a first attempt to set out its philosophy for the future. In the battle against inflation in 1975, it has begun to put it into practice and has put forward to government and to NEDC precise proposals for its own preferred solution.

THE CIVIL SERVICE

In the Civil Service too things are not what they were. The position in the social scale of senior civil servants has been eroded. A recent report on the service has noted areas of discontent and a general malaise heightened by the sharp and eroding effects of inflation. Yet immense efforts have been made to bring the service into line with modern circumstances. Management training, secondment to industry and a much strengthened Civil Service Department are some of the means employed to this end. Compared with the trade union movement or the employers' organisations, the Civil Service has retained more homogeneity, and it is still the best professional government service in the world.

To sum up it is surely not unrealistic to believe that the pressure of harsh events will create a situation where tripartite discussions between the TUC, CBI and government may start again, in the National Economic Development Council if not outside it, with a chance of success, if only the lessons of the past are not forgotten. From this approach could spring a new sense of unity of purpose in the national interest that could do much to restore Britain's industrial prosperity, provided that decisions at the top were backed by resolute action at shop floor level.

Chapter 6

MISSED OPPORTUNITIES

This chapter will examine two missed opportunities for developing practical collaboration between government and industry: the British National Export Council and the National Economic Development Council.

The BNEC has been replaced by a much more restricted operation, largely confined within the Department of Industry, but its history provides a hopeful example of what can be done to secure a united and bipartisan approach to a national problem under successive governments.

The NEDC continues as a functioning entity and is the base from which could be developed, if the will to do it were there, the kind of practical working collaboration that inspired the BNEC and that the nation needs for the future.

THE BRITISH NATIONAL EXPORT COUNCIL

The BNEC was founded by Edward Heath when he was President of the Board of Trade. It grew out of an export effort aimed at overseas markets that was fractionated and uncoordinated, a loose alliance of overseas chambers of trade and commerce and British export councils such as those for Europe and the western hemisphere. The concept was to knit the whole effort together and to provide it with a staff of able full-time officials. Control of policy was to be in the hands of the BNEC. This body was to be made up of industrialists, trade unionists, the nationalised industries, the City and ministers and senior civil servants representing the government departments involved—particularly the Department of Trade and the

Foreign Office. All these interests constituted a formidable body, but the system made sure that all the interests involved were committed to the task. Sir William McFadzean (now Lord McFadzean) was the first Chairman of the BNEC and handled it with his customary verve and charm.

I was invited by Edward Heath, the President of the Board of Trade, to form a Committee for Exports to the United States of America (CEUSA) and to be its first Chairman. This committee would take over the work of the Western Hemisphere Exports Council so far as the USA was concerned. It would be one of the more important committees of the BNEC of which I would become a member. I welcomed the opportunity of trying to make some contribution as a businessman to increasing Britain's exports at a time when an adverse balance of payments certainly justified a new approach to the whole problem of Britain's overseas trade. As a result I was involved in the overall work of the BNEC as well as in the specific area task of my own committee.

Much of the undoubted success of the BNEC sprang from the fact that the balance between authority and action was correctly struck. The council had the broad spread of authority for it represented all the industrial partners in Britain. The government too was generous in support, nobody more so than Harold Wilson when he became Prime Minister. Yet the action was left entirely to the businessmen and their BNEC staff. So although the businessmen sometimes acted first and consulted afterwards, this was a course of conduct well suited to the market needs of the time. So they got results, and ambassadors, senior civil servants and ministers all gave their support, even if the rules were sometimes forgotten. The trade unions and the nationalised industries were obviously not in a position to contribute to action in the same way, but their backing, which made the whole operation a national one, was invaluable. No export market was as important to Britain at that time as that of the United States. Yet that country also wanted to improve its balance of payments and it was therefore not easy to find an approach that justified, in American eyes, a major British trade drive across the whole of the United States. CEUSA had to find its own way through this problem and this is just what that first-class committee of able businessmen did. Every committee of the BNEC operated in this way and developed its own particular style which was suited to its market area. This flexibility enabled quick results to be achieved and avoided past mistakes where one export policy had been made to cover areas with totally diverse needs.

The example which I will quote of CEUSA at work was typical of the innovatory style adopted by all committees. It was an operation that could not have been mounted by government, in the time scale or with the informality that was necessary. It demonstrated the fact that, if government sets the policy frame, provides the essential backing and then lets free enterprise get on with the job, the nation gets the best of all possible results. My example is the arrangements made by CEUSA for the visit of His Royal Highness, the Duke of Edinburgh, to the USA and Canada in March 1966. The visit arose from His Royal Highness's interest in the charitable work of Variety Clubs International and the original arrangements for a visit to the Bahamas, the USA and Canada were made by officials of the Variety Club in London and the USA.

It seemed at the time to the businessmen on CEUSA, most of whom were actively engaged in promoting British exports to the USA and Canada, that this was an outstanding opportunity for the committee to organise a wide-ranging marketing sweep across the USA in conjunction with His Royal Highness's visit. The visit would be tied in with special promotions and events for British goods on the West Coast and in the Mid-West and New York. Prince Philip was kind enough to agree and those in the Variety Club concerned with his visit were equally co-operative about adding an additional dimension to his visit. So CEUSA was able to make a number of promotional arrangements which did a great deal to improve the image of British products in the most sophisticated market in the world.

The operation presented His Royal Highness with a number of challenging situations but, as always, he took them in his stride, modestly disclaiming the role of a commercial ambassador while fulfilling it with great skill. Donald Byford, the Vice-Chairman of CEUSA, and Geoffrey Knight of the British Aircraft Corporation were both particularly involved in the visit, as were other members of the committee and the President of Schweppes (USA) Limited, Commander Whitehead, who for some years had played an important role in promoting, not only that company's own products, but also British goods as a whole across the North American continent.

My first rendezvous with His Royal Highness, as Chairman of CEUSA, was at Palm Springs and my involvement in the venture started at a barbecue luncheon for sixty guests in the desert sunshine. That evening, after a polo match and an official welcome to Los Angeles for His Royal Highness, my committee was able to stage a special reception arranged by the British Consul-General and the British American Chamber of Commerce. This reception, at which 600 people were present, signalled the start of a special trade drive for Britain on the West Coast.

On the Monday a special exhibition of British cars had been arranged. Prince Philip agreed to open it and to present special certificates to local dealers who had played a major part in building up British car sales on the West Coast. I had to collect His Royal Highness at the 20th Century Fox Studios where, as part of his Variety Club programme, he lunched on the set in typical film star style and was presented by Bing Crosby with a Winchester repeating rifle. We just managed to get him away from Darryl Zanuck in time to open the car exhibition staged by the British American Chamber of Commerce in Los Angeles. The crowds exceeded all expectations and the cars and the exhibition were totally overwhelmed. Prince Philip had to climb from car to car over the stands to get round the exhibition and force his way through an enthusiastic crowd which almost got out of control. He might well have complained, but his calm remained quite unruffled as somehow he was got through the programme. However many British cars had been available, they could all have been sold on this occasion.

On Tuesday my rendezvous point was the O'Hare Airport, Chicago. His Royal Highness had a very lively press conference at which some pretty fast balls were bowled by all concerned. Next day CEUSA had arranged a formidable event for British goods in all the main stores in Chicago—the richest per capita market in the world. All the work for this intricate event had been successfully organised by the British American Chamber of Commerce in Chicago, which at that time was led by Wynn Ellis, a leading Chicago businessman and a good friend of Britain. He had done a very great deal to promote a real understanding in the city and state of Illinois of the fact that a greater flow of two-way trade between Britain and the USA must be to the advantage of both countries—a case certainly more effectively made by a prominent US citizen. This basis enabled us to pull out all the stops with large retail organisations like Marshall Fields and Sears Roebuck.

Wednesday started with an official call on Mayor Daly of Chicago, where His Royal Highness only just dodged an invitation to lead the St Patrick's Day parade. We then had a very intensive day visiting stores such as Marshall Fields and Sears Roebuck, which inflicted an immense amount of detailed trade ambassadorship on Prince Philip. The visiting was interspersed with a luncheon given by the British American Chamber of Commerce for all the leading Mid-West bankers and businessmen. Only when all this was over did he go on to his Variety Club work and to a banquet at the Conrad Hilton Hotel for over 1,000 people. Next day he opened a British export exhibition at O'Hare Airport and then flew to New York with Geoffrey Knight, in one of the British Air Corporation's BA111 jets which at that time were being sold to a number of American airlines. His Royal Highness went from the airport by helicopter to the Pan American Building. The following day he did more store visits in New York and had a special meeting with the British Exports Advisory Committee, which was a committee of prominent American businessmen who gave advice to British exporters on how to enter the US market. Afterwards, a luncheon organised by the British American Chamber of Commerce in New York had over 800 guests. In the evening he fitted in a reception given by the British Menswear Guild for another 300 prospective customers, organised by another member of CEUSA, Gerald Abrahams.

All in all, it was one of the most successful promotions that CEUSA ever handled in the United States, and its stimulus on members of the committee and on all those concerned with British exports to the United States lasted for a considerable time. It was very non-standard and quite successful, like most of the operations of the American committee, and it must have been rather a trial to the British Ambassador and his staff, but they never complained. When I resigned the chairmanship of CEUSA, having done my allotted span, in 1967, the then President of the Board of Trade said in a statement:

'The President has accepted Lord Watkinson's resignation with much regret. Between 1964 and 1966 British exports to the United States increased by 55% to £625m, an achievement which is a fair measure of the success of the Committee under Lord Watkinson's energetic leadership, in drawing to British industry's attention the great potential of the United States which remains our most important single export market.'

The credit was due certainly not to me but to all those, of whom His Royal Highness was a notable example, who were willing to give their time, knowledge and expertise to what they judged to be an important national objective. They did this in the true spirit of free enterprise, taking 'catch crops' wherever they could, in a way that a more formal organisation or even a governmental one could never have achieved. For example, only businessmen, aided by Commander Whitehead as the US link, could have set up the British Exports Marketing Advisory Committee. This committee was chaired by Teddy Whitehead and had a top level membership of American businessmen plus the advice of one of the most brilliant of the US advertising practitioners, David Ogilvy. It gave its expert advice free to all British businessmen who had a US export problem and published a very expert report on the market, which provided an excellent brief for all prospective new entrants to the market.

The BNEC therefore remains a unique example of what Britain can do, when it tries, in the way of bipartisan co-operation; businessmen co-operated with civil servants and members of the diplomatic service, and trade unionists co-operated with businessmen. The chairmen of the nationalised industries were involved and all the main political parties gave it their support. I shall never understand why in the end it proved impractical to continue it in this way. But it remains a very good example of the right continuing basis for collaboration between business, government and the trade unions. It is one of the strange whirligigs of politics, which so few managers understand, that the BNEC was founded by Edward Heath, was strongly supported by Harold Wilson and George Brown when Labour was in power, but was to receive a mortal blow from John Davies as Conservative Secretary of State for Trade and Industry.

There is a lesson to be learned here. By this time the BNEC had probably expended its original drive and novelty. It had also produced a good deal of tension, most of it creative, in the civil service and diplomatic service. It needed a very firm directive from the Secretary of State or Prime Minister to ensure that it was restructured to allow for much the same blend of entrepreneurism on the part of managers and the business world in its make-up and to see that it was not clutched back into the bosom of the Department of Industry. Lacking the directive, back it went and became what was then described as a 'low profile' operation. It became safe, secure and thoroughly defensible in Parliament and to select committees, but lost much of its vital spark. It could, of course, be reinvented, for the need for more British overseas trade has certainly not grown less, but this would now be difficult to achieve. The lesson surely is that the BNEC should not have been regarded as an innovation, to be wound up as soon as it needed an inevitable reshaping. The principle of working together in the cause of exports or anything else should have been regarded as a normal on-going policy. If it did nothing else it resulted in the government's getting the services of a lot of high-powered managers entirely without cost.

On a personal note, its epitaph so far as I was concerned was some words that I used in the autumn of 1966 at a luncheon at the Plaza Hotel in New York, when opening, at Gimbels store, a British Fortnight in that stimulating city. I said:

'Some of our young people's hair may be a little longer; some of our attractive girls' skirts may be a little shorter; some of our attempts to denigrate ourselves in public a little more violent than they were a decade ago. Nonetheless we are still the same nation that stood alone against what seemed overwhelming odds in 1940. We are still the same nation that had the guts and farsightedness to turn an Empire into a Commonwealth, despite all the problems that a Commonwealth presents. And we are the nation that accounts for over 9% of total world trade and whose exports as a proportion of our gross national product are higher than West Germany's, 50% more than Japan's, and three times the level in the United States.'

Ten years later all this effort seems almost irrelevant—the more is the pity. Somehow there is a need to reinvent, not the BNEC itself, but the spirit of drive and co-operation that lay behind the operation and gave it its driving force. This is the continuing lesson of the missed opportunity of the BNEC.

'NEDDY' AND THE 'LITTLE NEDDIES'

Now I will turn to a much more important and fundamental issue: the National Economic Development Council. The BNEC is an interesting example of an 'approach' to the problem, but the NEDC is at the heart of the problem itself. Because of this council's importance to the solution of the nation's problems, it is worth studying the history of its operations in some detail. Again I can vouch for the facts from personal experience. I was a member of Harold Macmillan's Cabinet at the time it gave approval to the NEDC concept when it was laid before it by Selwyn Lloyd as Chancellor in March 1962. As always, the stop-go nature of the British economy was causing the whole Cabinet grave concern. After much consideration and discussion, the Cabinet was unanimous in a belief that somehow some new way had to be found to bring together government, trade unionists and industrialists in a setting that would focus the real needs of the economic climate of the day. At first sight the concept of such a council, to meet under the Chancellor's chairmanship, did not look like the Draconian instrument that some members of the Cabinet were seeking. Yet the more the Cabinet looked at it, the more it seemed to be the most promising initiative that the government could take at that time. So in fact it has turned out to be, for the council's powers of survival have proved to be considerable, even if it has not yet fully played the significant part in steering the economy that its initiators hoped for. 'Neddy' (the cosiness of the nickname is a hopeful sign) has survived through six parliaments and under four prime ministers. To quote its present Director General, Sir Ronald McIntosh: through twelve turbulent years it has remained 'an island of consensus in an increasingly divided country'.

What then is Neddy, and why has it survived when the Department of Economic Affairs, the Industrial Re-organisation Corporation, the Prices and Incomes Board and the Industrial Relations Court have failed? Why does it still command the attention of leaders of industry and of the trade unions, even if its direct influence on the government's economic policy is still less than its original instigators hoped? The answers are: primarily because it is what Ronald McIntosh so aptly called it, that is, 'an island of consensus'—a place where, because it is there and because it is neutral and fair, the three estates of the realm can meet and talk to one another, free of the constraints of public positions of conflicting policy. It would be quite wrong, however, to look at Neddy as merely a meeting place. The council normally has the Chancellor in the chair, with the secretaries of state for Trade and for Employment and other ministers present. The Confederation of British Industry is represented by its President and Director General, and the Trades Union Congress by the Chairman of its Economic Committee and its General Secretary. Together with representatives of the City and the nationalised industries, these make a powerful group of men round the council table. As a forum for the discussion of economic and industrial policy by such men it must have influence, but it has suffered from a lack of disclosure by the Treasury (which tends to tell Neddy only what it wants it to know) and from a lack of any real decision-making power. So the NEDC will have to acquire new authority if it is to play a more significant and unifying role.

Below the council are the 'little Neddies', the Economic Development Councils. These are structured in the same way as the NEDC, with each EDC representing a sector of private industry. They have no executive power, but they have developed a considerable talent for examining their own industry and producing reports covering a wide range of subjects. Their performance has been uneven, as would be expected, and some have hardly got off the ground. Yet the principle is right and largely accepted. So if a strengthened NEDC came into being, it would not have to invent its sectoral machinery; this already exists in the little Neddies, imperfect in some ways as they are.

The NEDC is served by the Economic Development Office. This provides planning and logistic backing for the NEDC's

Director General and is responsible to the three Neddy partners. It was a very sensible idea to give Neddy its own 'department'. Here again is the framework for a more powerful and viable instrument, which would clearly need an independent source of information, statistics and policy-forming elements. The framework is there, but if the NEDC is to become the chosen instrument around which can be created a new industrial and economic unity, then there are a number of operational problems to be solved. First, if Neddy is to become more of a decision-taking body, its relationship with Parliament will need to be considered. Perhaps there should be a counterpart in Parliament to Neddy. There might be an all-party committee on trade and industry, for example, which could examine investment problems on a reasonably bipartisan basis. Then there is its relationship with the other planning and executive areas of government. It might be predicted, on the basis of past experience, that the National Enterprise Board will in due course go the way of the Department of Economic Affairs, the Industrial Re-organisation Corporation, the Prices and Incomes Board and other interventionist bodies. So long as it continues to exist it must not be allowed to interfere with NEDC procedures or the tripartite approach. Then there is the question of planning agreements, which raises the whole issue of how decisions taken in the NEDC at national level can be explained and implemented at sectoral level. The EDCs have no executive power or machinery for the implementation of decisions. In the French system of economic planning, companies are entitled to opt 'in' or 'out' of a sectoral plan on the basis of their own commercial decision. This in Britain would raise awkward problems of creating chosen instruments and might give companies which opted to carry through NEDC/ government policies by agreement an unfair advantage over those, probably the smaller companies, which did not. Nor do the EDCs at the moment cover the whole of industry, and if they did there would still be a need to relate their work to the needs of trade associations and individual firms.

Behind this is an unresolved problem of how to relate the drive and discipline of the market economy to the kind of overall national policy which the full use of the NEDC and EDCs would begin to generate. No political party would today want to return to previous concepts of a national plan based on a target growth figure. Yet a new lead from Neddy would obviously involve the creation of a new industrial and economic planning framework. The CBI has given a great deal of thought to the whole problem and the pressure of events is likely to cause the TUC and government to follow the same course.

THE 4 PER CENT SYNDROME

This is not the place to trace the detailed history of the NEDC since 1962, but together with the Department of Economic Affairs and other bodies it has been associated with what may be described as the 4 per cent syndrome. Under successive governments, both Conservative and Labour, repeated attempts have been made to achieve a genuine 4 per cent growth rate. The first task of the NEDC under its first Director General, Sir Robert Shore, was to examine the implications of a 4 per cent growth rate for the economy. Reginald Maudling as Chancellor had to bear the political brunt of first taking the brakes off growth and then seeing them almost automatically reimposed by balance-of-payments difficulties. This did not deter George Brown, who in the national plan again returned to the target of a 4 per cent growth rate. But again, balance-of-payments difficulties forced the abandonment of the national plan and with it any great belief in planning for growth, in this sense. In quite different circumstances, Anthony Barber tried his own version of a dash of growth, but again defeat was caused by balance-of-payments problems. This time defeat came as a result more of the oil producers' policy than of other factors.

Yet 4 per cent growth per annum would not be regarded as a very testing target by managers in normal circumstances.

So part of this analysis must take account of why, under successive governments, it has proved impossible to achieve this target on a national basis. To endeavour to provide a clue to the answer, I cannot do better than to quote from the 'Lubbock Memorial Lecture' given by the Director General of the NEDC, Sir Ronald McIntosh, towards the end of 1974. He said, referring to the limitations under which the NEDC and indeed the whole concept of national planning were labouring:

'Moreover, of the three parties only the Government has real power. The TUC and CBI are representative and not executive bodies. They can try to persuade their members to take a course of action but they cannot commit them. There are immense problems in communicating with rank and file trade unionists and managers, who understandably find it difficult to put their own individual difficulties into a national context. And as someone said at last week's NEDC, where information is poor the extremists take over.

'Thus people on the Council may understand that our present economic situation calls for a big switch of resources from private consumption to exports and productive investment. But the man down the line who sees his standard of living cut and his job threatened will take a less altruistic view. So the leaders of both the TUC and CBI are subject to pressures from below which they ignore at their peril, for if they leave their members too far behind the result will be loss of support and the setting up of alternative, more radical institutions at the grass roots level.

'But the tripartite involvement faces difficulties because of Government attitudes also. Ministers and their advisers in this country habitually shy away from open discussion of the assumptions and predictions on which economic policy is based and dislike the restrictions on their freedom of manoeuvre which tripartite involvement in policy making could bring about. In this respect we are much worse off than USA or Germany, for example. The Council faces an additional problem which is rapidly growing in importance. This is the problem of how to communicate the results of its deliberations to the people in industry who actually take the decisions that improve productivity and performance. This is especially relevant to the shopfloor. So far the attitude of the trade union movement to Neddy has been friendly and benevolent. But the movement is rapidly changing and the pressures on trade union officials, who sit on EDCs and working parties, have grown prodigiously. Nowadays, when even members of the General Council of the TUC may be regarded by their members as elitist, Neddy will have to work hard to avoid the twin dangers of alienation and indifference.'

THE PEOPLE DECIDE

It is at least conceivable that the failure to achieve real growth, undispersed by a corresponding increase in productivity and efficiency, has been largely due to these causes. Somehow the whole weight and drive of the nation has never been harnessed to the cause of genuine growth. Everybody has wanted to take more out of the pot than he has been willing to put in, and this implies a major failure in understanding on the part of ordinary men and women in all walks of life. Appeals from politicians of all parties, productivity schemes, output incentives, export drives, stop and go in the economy—nothing seems to have really brought it home to the citizens of Britain that they have been living far beyond their means and exertions in these postwar years. Yet such an attitude is understandable. Earnings have, on the whole, kept pace with inflation for the majority of the population; those who have fallen behind, such as sections of the middle class, are not significant in terms of votes. Politicians have warned, but they have also talked about 'never having had it so good' and the 'value of the pound in one's pocket'.

Britain understood the implications of an enemy on the

French shore, but has never begun to understand the significance of economic disaster, long threatened but never more than a cloud on the horizon. Management must take its share of the blame for the situation particularly in times when people will increasingly accept that facts are true only when they see them in the context of their own immediate circumstances. It may have been unwise to commit the nation to achieving the simultaneous goals of full employment, stable prices and rising standards of living, but these have been promised time and time again by all political parties and the lack of full performance has clearly not been too alarming for most people. So the British have stumbled on, uncaring for anything outside their own short-term and selfish objectives. Now only hard times can provide a corrective, but even in such circumstances there will need to be a greater degree of understanding of the real problems by the people if Britain is to survive. So a study of corrective action must start where it has to have its first results, that is, in ordinary people's lives.

The outline of a blueprint for industrial survival has to be traced from where it must all begin—at the roots of society. The machinery is needed as well, but in the end it is the people who decide and it is the people who must therefore clearly understand the facts against which decisions have to be made.

Chapter 7

THE WAY BACK: A NEW APPROACH TO INVOLVEMENT IN DECISION MAKING

COMPANY AFFAIRS

Far-sighted industrialists and professional men have for some years past been deeply troubled at the future prospects, as they see them, for free enterprise. As a result of representations to the Confederation of British Industry, in 1971 it was decided by the then President, Sir John Partridge, that it was an appropriate moment to take a new and detailed look at the whole question of company affairs. So the Company Affairs Committee of the CBI began its work in the spring of 1972. At John Partridge's invitation I agreed to become its Chairman, making only the stipulation, readily accepted, that the committee should be completely unfettered in anything that it might decide to recommend.

The committee was made up of leading figures from accountancy, the law and industry. It had strong City representation and the formal backing of the Governor of the Bank of England. Its interim report was debated in the CBI's Regional Councils, at area meetings up and down the country, in the Smaller Firms Council and at a CBI national conference. The committee also held discussions with the European Economic Community, the Trades Union Congress and the Conservative government which was then in the process of producing a White Paper on company law. Chairing such a committee was a stimulating and exacting task. It seemed to me, as one who believed deeply in the importance of management as a profession, that I could not put my name to recommendations that I was unable to implement in my own business sphere. So I faced a challenge. Persuading the institutions of the City of London to consider their proper responsibilities as major shareholders in British industry was difficult enough, but even more important to me was the task of persuading my own business colleagues both inside and outside my own business that they too had to face major change.

The proposals that follow, for closer involvement of employees in decision making, are for operators rather than theorists, but before they are examined in detail it may be helpful to say something of the background of the Company Affairs Committee. The committee spoke nothing but the hard truth when it said:

> 'Business today operates in a time of change. It must therefore show itself capable of the degree of evolution and self-reform necessary to cope efficiently with the new circumstances in which it has to operate.'

In the end the committee's findings were unanimous and the report was approved with equal unanimity by the CBI's Grand Council. Resultant action was disappointingly slow and not nearly so unanimous. As Bernard Hollowood wrote in the *Daily Telegraph* in a light-hearted piece about a fairly mythical boardroom:

> ' "I'll tell you what I'll do," said the Chairman. "I'll write to Lord Watkinson and ask him to expand on his statement. Then if you all agree we'll discuss it again in a year or two's time. Agreed?" '

Yet the pressures for change were there for those who were wise enough to recognise them. In Europe the Commission of the EEC was pressing forward with company reform and Finn Gundelach, the commissioner responsible, made it very plain to me and to other members of CBI that he saw revolutionary change in this sphere as inevitable. The industrial democracy working party of the TUC, under the chairmanship of Sir Sydney Green (now Lord Green) of the National Union of Railwaymen, was pressing for a British solution similar to that applied by the West German government, where trade unionists claimed 50 per cent of the places in the supervisory boards of larger companies. TUC opinion at this stage was still divided, and British directors and managers could have seized the initiative here and in Europe if they had known how to do it.

British management, in its collective sense, was slow to realise that to manage its own affairs successfully was now not enough. The problems external to business would not go away and management had to regard the solution of national problems as an essential part of its management task. If management in industry was understandably reluctant to face its outside problems, the City just did not want to know about them at all. Again this was only too understandable. City 'managers' claimed, with some justice, to be expert in the selection and management of investment portfolios, not in the management of industrial enterprises. 'Sell and go away' was their remedy for impending trouble, not 'stay and sort it out', as an industrial manager had to do. Yet as the holders of over 50 per cent of the equity in British companies, their influence could not be ignored.

It would be unfair, even now, to claim that no progress has been made. In British industry there is a greater ferment of creative thought at present than ever before. Hundreds of companies, large and small, have experimented in the field of better communications and better consultation with their employees. The Commission of the EEC has been persuaded that its Fifth Directive on company board structure must be reconsidered. The City has set up an institutional shareholders, watch-dog committee that has at least some teeth. Yet the hard experience of my political years warned me that the rate of progress was not fast enough to meet the challenge of the times

—a belief fully indicated by the variety of legislative solutions now enacted or proposed in this area. I, together with many others, tried to preach the necessity of change on television and in the press. In the end I came to the conclusion that the best contribution that I could make at that time was to pioneer a solution in my own company, in the hope that it would be both an example and a challenge to other industrialists.

THE CADBURY SCHWEPPES EXPERIMENT

I do not here put the Cadbury Schweppes experiment forward as an exact blueprint to be copied; each company must tailor its own solution to its own problem. I put it forward in all seriousness and sincerity as a clue to the way back to industrial prosperity for Britain. Such prosperity must be rebuilt on the foundations of consent and involvement on the part of all the employees and, in the end, all the citizens of the country. In my initial approach to my board colleagues and later to the management and shop stewards, I took as my brief the eighth principle of corporate conduct from the Company Affairs Report. This said:

'The Board has to forge closer relationships with its employees towards a common purpose. This is in the interests of its shareholders as well as its employees. The main purpose must be to secure a wider participation in the processes of decision making on the part of all employees.'

At first the Cadbury Schweppes board, like most other boards with whom I have discussed the problem, saw only the risks and difficulties. But the company had one great advantage over many other companies: Schweppes and Cadbury both had behind them a long tradition of good personal relationships at all levels. This had been built on after the merger, for in the inevitably difficult postmerger sorting out a new initiative in companywide discussions had been decided on. This was based on personal visits by the Chairman and Deputy Chairman to all major factories and sites for frank informal discussions with all employees on the shopfloor. The purpose of the exercise was ostensibly to discuss the published annual and half-year profit figures. In fact, these were used as a peg on which to hang a wide-ranging discussion on the progress of the company.

As Chairman, I went round the company in the autumn of each year to discuss the half-year figures. As Deputy Chairman, Adrian Cadbury (now Chairman) went round to discuss the annual figures in the spring of each year. Informality was the keynote of the whole proceedings. Each plant manager made his own arrangements to suit his own local circumstances. Sometimes it would be shop stewards and managers together; at other sites these groups were separated. Everywhere discussions and questions were free and unfettered. Some points which we two had to face may be useful to those who would like to consider this method as a 'way in' to closer relationships:

1   First walk round the plant and be seen. Meet shop stewards and shopfloor management as you go round. Then lunch in the works canteen with stewards and managers informally selected, holding the meeting immediately after lunch.
2   Open the meeting by a short resumé of company affairs.
3   Always talk about 'cash', not profits. What matters to employees is the forward order position, capital investment, job security and the progress of 'their' part of the business. This is always more clearly understood if explained in terms of cash, rather than remote balance sheet or profit-and-loss figures.
4   Devote most of the time to informal question and answer sessions. Do the answering yourself, for it is you they have come to hear. Refer the question to the works management only on detailed and strictly local issues.

Such meetings can be organised on a totally *ad hoc* basis, but there are dangers in this. Mass meetings of the whole plant are useless, unless the total numbers are under 100, and the selection of representatives on a random basis can lead to jealousy and misunderstanding. So the concept of top level visits presupposes a plant council structure, and it is the members of the plant council who are the hard core of the meeting. In Cadbury Schweppes this was the practice adopted. Plant councils were 'joint councils': in other words, 50 per cent shop stewards and 50 per cent management. There are thus two important points for those who would base their organisation on this kind of meeting:

1 There must be an organised, functioning plant council.
2 If the council does not represent management (and some do not), other means must be found of involving management in the meeting. It is quite fatal to appear to bypass management in any approach to employees. Managers are paid to manage and the whole structure of the company depends on the management chain of command being effective and efficient. So do not under any circumstances bypass the managers.

At these plant meetings it became obvious that many of the problems discussed in their local context had been decided at company level a considerable time before they were ever known at plant level. This circumstance led on quite naturally to consideration of the next step, namely, an experiment that would develop a structure that would link company decision-making more effectively with the shopfloor. Without this direct link, meetings at plant level could never do more than generally inform; consultation or participation would always be barred by the sheer timescale of events.

CONSULTATION WITH THE BOARD

The problem was how to set up a controlled experiment that would give the board and all employees a means of judging whether it was possible to hold direct discussions between the board and representatives of the employees. I believed that such discussions would be a valuable bridge between the top and bottom of the company and I hoped that they would also provide a path of promotion from the shopfloor to the boardroom. How to start the scheme off, without irrevocable commitment, was the problem. It might well fail and in this case make relationships worse rather than better. After a good deal of thought it was decided that the right initiative would be to send a personal letter of invitation from me, as Chairman, to a carefully selected number of employees who were known to have played a leading part in the joint consultative system. Roughly 50 per cent were shop stewards and 50 per cent shopfloor management. The letter invited them to come to London in March 1973, to meet the board of the company, immediately after it had announced the preliminary profit figures for the past year.

The practical arrangements were to hold the board on the preliminary figures in the morning, announce them to the Stock Exchange at noon and meet the employee representatives immediately after lunch in the company conference room at Connaught Place head office. I took the chair and James Forbes, the finance director, gave a simple and non-technical run-down on the figures that had just been announced. I then explained that this was a purely experimental meeting, at which nobody was asked to commit himself. We would see how it all worked out as we went along. Perhaps the purposes of the meeting, as they emerged, were best summarised in the words of one of the leading shop stewards present. He said:

'Chairman, we understand that if this experiment proceeds, you will give us all the information that we need to understand the business. You will then see that we understand the information. We shall then consider it and in due course come back to you with our own ideas upon it. We accept that you are not likely to agree with many of the proposals that we make, but we do expect that where you do not agree you will give us clear reasons for not going along with it.'

I was happy to agree on behalf of the board that this was exactly what we had in mind. As the meeting proceeded it became apparent that both the board and the invited employees felt that the whole experience was well worthwhile. The questions were penetrating but fair and most of the board members were involved in the dialogue.

Success owed a great deal to the selection of those invited and to the general briefing that they had been given about the purpose of the meeting. Here we could not have achieved anything but for the efforts of Frank Hamer, the company personnel director. To him is due much of the success of the Cadbury Schweppes experiment. The lesson to be learned is the total necessity of having personnel relationships effectively represented at board level in this kind of experiment.

The March meeting decided that it would like to carry out a further experiment in connection with the interim figures in September. This would give all concerned a chance, during the intervening months, to report back and to assess the reaction of the company as a whole. At the September meeting, duly held, all seemed to have gone well. So it seemed appropriate to me that now a further challenge should be issued. If the experiment was to continue, it now had to be institutionalised. The meetings could not go on by invitation; they would have to be related to the company structure of joint consultation. It was not for the board to decide but for those present representing the employees. The board had opened the door; it was for the 'company' to push through it if it so desired. It was soon clear at the September meeting that no one wanted to end the experiment. So it was agreed that a working party should be set up, from those present, to plan proposals for future co-operation between the board and the employees on the basis of 'a growing degree of participation in the processes leading up to decision making'.

The working party would have the assistance of one main board director, Frank Hamer, but it would be entirely independent and would take its own responsibility for discussion and consultation throughout the company. It would be chaired by Ken Marriott, a personnel manager. In due course it would come back to the board with firm proposals for institutionalising the informal relations built up at the first two meetings.

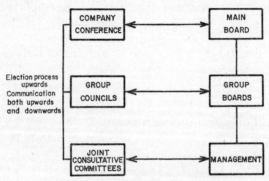

Figure 1   Joint Committee Structure

Much hard and patient work had to follow. Some opposition had to be overcome and the opponents were given every opportunity to air their views. The trade union position had to be carefully studied. I made sure, for example, that Jack Jones, as General Secretary of the company's main union, the Transport and General Workers' Union, knew in broad outline what was going on, but I was most careful not to consult him. This was a 'company', not a 'trade union', experiment. However, it was made known that long-standing and firmly established collective-bargaining arrangements with the unions would in no way be affected by the proposals and would remain outside them. So by December 1973 it was possible to write in the company magazine:

'Regular face-to-face discussions between employee representatives—including management, sales and distribution—and Main Board Directors may begin with the first meeting of the new Company Conference in March 1974.'

It was called a 'company conference' to distinguish it from the joint consultative committees and group councils that formed the rest of the joint committee structure, which schematically was presented as in Figure 1.

This structure represented the 30,000 UK employees of the company in the following proportions:

Group or Section	Number of Representatives
Confectionery group	8
Tea and foods group	6
Drinks group	5
Health and chemical products group	4
Company services	1
Overseas group (UK employees)	1
Kenco and Kardomah	1
Concentrates and essences	1
Cadbury Schweppes specialities	1

As Ken Marriott, the working party chairman, said:

'This is only the beginning. We recognise the variety of employee interests which sometimes clash with the Company and sometimes with one another. But we hope that we can all learn to understand and widen the areas of joint interest which are essential for the well being of the Company, its employees and the Community.'

Behind this achievement lay an immense amount of detailed briefing and education provided by the company for both managers and employees. Initial instruction was carried out at the company's own management training centre, 'The Beeches', at Bournville. All shop steward members of the company conference and some from the group councils were sent on a

week's course in business management at a Midlands management school, in company time and at the company's expense.
A particular effort was made to bring all managers into the
picture, as their enthusiastic support was essential for the
success of the total operation. A complete brief was provided
by the personnel department for all groups and divisions.
This was accompanied by slides and was also fully discussed
with all directors, including those below main board level. The
company at this time had some sixty directors in this category,
and they were all given a special briefing at the two-day
chairman's conference which I held each year at a management
centre near Nottingham for all directors. The captions to some
of the slides provide for the brief summing up of the picture, as
it was presented not only to managers but also to all employees.
They were as follows:

What is participation?
Participation means a management style which considers it
important to communicate *to* all employees, to consult *with*
them, and to allow them to *take an increasing part in decision-
making processes.*

What forms does it take?
Participation in the ownership of the business.
Participation in the decision-making processes at the level of
one's own job.
Participation through institutions in the decision-making
processes of the business.

Why have it?
1 *Developments in society:*
Increasing levels of education.
Growing affluence.
Lack of exposure to hardships such as heavy unemployment
or poverty.
Availability of greater information due to influence of mass
media.

2 *Developments in industry:*
 Demands for increased status, greater job security, better
   working conditions, pay.
 Conflict and unrest.
 Demands for a greater voice in decision-making processes.
3 *Influence of the EEC:*
 Draft Directive No. 5.

*Objectives of the working party in recognising the growing desire of
employees for more involvement in the decision-making processes of the
company:*
1 To make proposals for the further development of mutual
  understanding in the wide-ranging and often complex
  issues facing the main board.
2 To make proposals for the representative structure for
  employee contact with the main board.
3 To make these recommendations by early 1974 as a basis for
  wider discussion through the company's established joint
  consultative machinery, leading to agreed arrangements for
  operation from the spring of 1974.

Recommendations of the working party (see Figure 2):
Establishment of the company conference.
Establishment of group councils.
Establishment of joint consultative committees.

To meet this, recommendations were made with regard to:
Size
Representation
Election versus selection
Agenda
Frequency of meetings
Communications
Education and training.

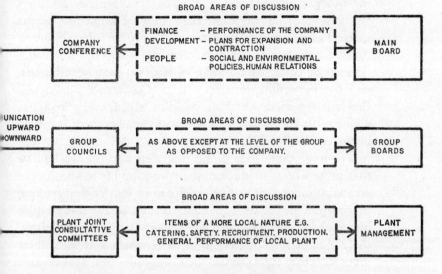

Figure 2   The Three-level Consultation System

In my statement to stockholders of 28 March 1974 I was able to inform them on behalf of the board of the precise steps that the company was going to take. I said:

'I am delighted to report that in response to an initiative from those involved in our joint consultation machinery, your Board has agreed to the setting up of four Group Councils which cover our main operating Groups in the UK. Membership of these Councils is on an elected basis from Works Councils. From these four Group Councils approximately 30 representatives will be elected to a completely new body, the "Company Conference". This body therefore represents, on a democratic basis, all those who work with us in the UK. Its first Chairman, Frank Hamer, who is responsible for Personnel matters, is a member of your Board.

'Stockholders should know that this statement and the accompanying figures will be discussed in detail with the Company Conference on the same day as they are issued to

the Stock Exchange and to stockholders. Further meetings
will follow so that the Conference may be briefed on major
matters of policy such as investment, product development,
profit forecasts and other matters. It is agreed that issues
covered by collective bargaining, such as wage negotiations,
will not be within the scope of the Conference which will
thus not supersede our long standing and friendly arrangements with the trade unions whose members are involved
in the work of the Conference.

'We have taken this pioneering step because we believe
that those who give much of their working life to serving the
company have a right to participate in its decision-making
processes. This "share" obviously cannot be the same as the
financial stake held by stockholders and in no way diminishes
the rights of stockholders to elect directors and fulfil their
other statutory rights under the Companies Act. It is in your
Board's view very much in the long term interests of stockholders that employees should participate to an increasing
extent in the processes of decision making on which the
profitability of your company depends'.

I very much looked forward to the first meeting of the company
conference. Time was running out for me, so far as Cadbury
Schweppes was concerned. The Company Affairs Committee
had recommended that chairmen should not enjoy too much
security of tenure and should consider retirement as Chairman
at sixty-five or fairly soon afterwards. I intended to live up to
what the committee had said. So I was delighted when the
conference went off successfully and established the Cadbury
Schweppes experiment on the correct basis of an initiative
from the shopfloor, supported by management and the board.
It also met my other point and provided a clear channel of
promotion from the shopfloor to the boardroom. Frank Hamer,
the first Chairman of the Company Conference, was on the
board. His successor, who would be elected from the conference,
would also have the right to a board seat.

WORKER DIRECTORS

This is the right method of tackling the difficult problem of so-called 'worker directors'. Very few directors in Britain today do not fall into this category. One would have to return to prewar days, when some chairmen's desire was to fill their boards with 'names' rather than men of proved ability, to find any substantial body of directors who were not, in effect, professional managers at board level. So what is being discussed is not the qualities of the present-day director but his class background. Worker directors, in left wing terms, are of exactly the same class as the 'names' of earlier years. They are men who will be nominated to boards because of their position in a trade union or political party, not because of their business knowledge or ability.

Some confusion has been caused by a misunderstanding of the West German board practice and the EEC's original draft Fifth Directive, which was largely based upon it. The West German two-tier board structure derives more from the Allied Control Commission of the late 1940s than from industrial practice. The controlling board, which has the prime duty of appointing and monitoring the work of the executive board, was a device invented by that commission. Its purpose was to avert a postwar growth of West German companies which would follow the prewar tradition of vast industrial empires, such as Krupps, wielding national political and industrial power. With West German industry largely owned by the banks, rather than by private shareholders as in Britain, the device fitted German industrial practice. When the demand for worker representation arose it was obviously easiest to provide for trade union representation at supervisory level. In many areas, the control exercised over the company by the supervisory board is minimal and the controlling board is largely a facade that meets the requirements of the banks and the West German trade unions for a degree of insight into company financial affairs without management involvement.

Taking account of the totally different requirements of British company law and practice, with a unitary board directly responsible to shareholders, it was not difficult to persuade the EEC Commission that the draft Fifth Directive must be replaced in due course by proposals that will take more account of differing company structure in countries such as West Germany, France and Britain. This did not stop some activists in the socialist party and the British trade unions from adopting the concept as a convenient way of recommending plans that would pack boards with trade union nominees, who would recognise a responsibility only to those who had placed them there and not to shareholders. Things cannot stay as they are; pressures from the EEC as well as at home will see to that. Managers must seek to play a significant role in eventual decisions. They will, after all, have to implement the decisions reached, and it is important that these are based on common sense.

A British board is a unitary body with a collective legal and managerial responsibility for manning the business in the interests of its owners, that is, the shareholders. To be a useful member of a modern board requires expert practical knowledge of the business, as far as executive directors are concerned, and of finance, accountancy, politics, the market or some other aspect of business life important to the company, as far as 'outside' or non-executive directors are concerned. It also requires a total commitment to the interests of the shareholders. Today, members of trade unions will qualify for the first category if they have been employees of the company for a reasonable period of time, or for the second if their trade union experience is relevant to the interests of the company. In the first case they should join the board by reason of the ability they have displayed in joint consultation and participation in the processes of decision making at board level. Companies that now have a top tier of joint consultation at this level need do no more than select from this area when they have board vacancies. Companies should also consider the trade union field—as well as the fields of industry, the professions or politics—when they are looking for 'outside' non-executive directors.

Legislation laying down precise formulae for board membership will do more harm than good to what must be a slow but steady process of evolution. Difficult questions of divided loyalty may well arise, and to my personal knowledge many trade unionists are well aware that to cross the line from collective bargaining to management at board, or any other, level is a step that needs very serious thought on behalf of all those concerned. All a government that means well by industry needs to do is to take negative power to enable it to 'satisfy itself that the proper processes of consultation and participation are being carried out through the appropriate machinery'. Governments that wish to curry political favour with one unheeding pressure group or another may well take action that could set back for a generation the sound growth of true worker participation in industry at board level. Meantime, companies will be wise to press on with their own experimentation and not to wait for government. This is what was done in my time as Chairman of Cadbury Schweppes.

The Times said about this experiment, in an article after the first meeting between the company conference and the board:

'Last week Lord Watkinson, Chairman of Cadbury Schweppes, with every appearance of equanimity, took some of his own medicine or perhaps it could better be called tonic.

'As Chairman of the CBI's company affairs committee he was responsible last year for the production of a report on "The Responsibilities of the British Public Company", and in particular he personally wrote the section dealing with "The Company and its Employees". In this section he recommended "the development of methods allowing a wider degree of participation in the processes of decision making throughout British Industry".

'Cadbury Schweppes has now followed that advice and on

Wednesday the first formal meeting of the company conference took place in London.

'Mr Desmond Brown, a shop steward from Fry's chocolate
factory at Somerdale, near Bristol, said he saw the value of
the company conference in enabling employees to meet the
board on matters of importance which were outside the
scope of normal negotiating machinery. The work-force
would have a chance "to have a say before the board have
finalised their conclusions on matters which vitally affect
us".'

My friend of many years, Victor Feather (now Lord Feather),
kindly came to the inaugural luncheon for the delegates of the
first company conference. He congratulated everyone on what
had been achieved and afterwards commented to me, as one
Yorkshireman to another, 'Well Harold, if you get stabbed in
the back fewer times, it will all be worth while'. I hope and
believe Cadbury Schweppes will do a great deal better than
this. More important, I believe that this and other experiments
will show the way back to a more soundly based prosperity for
many other companies and perhaps for the nation itself.

THE WIDER SCENE

Finally, let us examine the Cadbury Schweppes experiment
in the light of progress made by other companies and to see it
against the national problem of social and industrial relationships in a changing society. Few managers today would quarrel
with the concept that successful decision making has to carry
employees' willing participation. This is also a lesson increasingly
impressed by events on politicians, industrialists and trade
union leaders. The question is: Are guidelines to be found in
increased participation in industrial decision making that can
be significant in a national context?

Certainly many other companies, large and small, are seeing
it this way. ICI, one of the pioneers of a consultative system,

and Scott Bader, a pioneer of co-ownership, are no longer
blazing their respective trails alone. GKN, Plessey and IPC, to
name only a few, are all experimenting with their own solutions
leading to a better understanding of the basis of decision making
at board level. But to date few companies have completed the
total package that offers a secure foundation for the way back to
growth and prosperity for Britain. As Cadbury Schweppes has
come as near to it as most, perhaps I may presume to speak
not only from conviction but also from some degree of practical
experience, when I sum up what has to be done in the field of
improving British social relationships.

A NEW APPROACH TO SOCIAL AND
INDUSTRIAL RELATIONSHIPS

Policy in this area has, above all, to be made by people, for
people and about people—not by figures on a remote national
stage, not for purely sectional interests, but by and for *all* the
people. Only in this way can the criterion of current change be
fulfilled, which is that individuals will react only to circumstances that touch their own lives. As British society is becoming
increasingly managed and is largely business-centred, this
new social and industrial relationship must be created by the
managers in society. Today the profession of management is
not restricted to business and commerce, if it ever was. Managers
today exercise their skills in the professions, the civil service,
local government, the trade unions and national government.
Every kind of enterprise needs management, and the creed for
managers must be that they recognise that everyone who works
with them must be led by good and ethical management to
understand the facts and to participate in the judgement on
those facts from which management decisions are made.
This does not mean that managers, in the final analysis, do not
have to manage and to take their own exposed management
decisions. It does mean that they have to realise that such
decisions can only be successfully implemented if those whom

they affect have gone along with the fact-finding and consultative processes that have led up to decision making.

Managers will not find themselves without backing and encouragement in their task. Their own institute, the British Institute of Management, has taken its stand on a code of best practice that is based on the need for more ethical and participative management. The City, through its City Company Law Committee, welcomes greater employee participation as a way to improve the efficiency and profitability of the private sector. The CBI Employment Policy Committee takes a similar view.

The Industry Act 1975 and the official inquiry into worker participation and Board structure are proof of the validity of the warnings that managers must put their own house in order or face legislative change of an uncompromising nature.

THE SOLUTION

This study of postwar British industry has identified the major areas where things have gone wrong. The most important of these is that of social and industrial relationships in a changing society. What should be learned from past mistakes in this area? Surely it is that political or industrial tinkering at the top is now totally irrelevant to the real size and nature of the national problem. The solution has to be found where all successful revolutions have started, that is, at the roots of society. Managers have a vital task to play, for their sphere of the management of people, for people and by people is the point where the way back to true prosperity in Britain must start.

If only British industry as a whole would begin to follow the path charted in broad outline in the original 'Company Affairs' report, a path already being successfully followed by many companies, then a major step would be taken towards soundly based industrial recovery. This necessary foundation at plant and company levels will remain essential whatever legislative changes are imposed from Whitehall. So will a continual willingness on the part of Government, CBI, and TUC to work together for the industrial recovery of Britain within the context of a long-term national plan.

Chapter 8

THE WAY BACK: A BASIS FOR A NATIONAL PLAN

A FAIR BALANCE IN THE MIX

If management gives of its best in leadership towards a more involved and participative society, it will have done its part towards laying the necessary foundation for a return to genuine prosperity. It is beyond management's capability to build on that foundation, but this first stage is essential to eventual success. Two additional criteria need to be met by a recovery plan. It needs (a) to correct the present incompatibility between the industrial and the political approach, and (b) to ensure that the scale of operation is within the national capability.

Because the mixed economy—part state, part free enterprise —is accepted in Britain, the balance of the mix has not been challenged as it should have been. Nor has enough thought been given to the dangers when a nation, no longer rich and powerful in world terms, plays party politics to a degree that renders coherent industrial decision making almost impossible. Unless Britain can achieve, now, a fair and stable balance in the mix of its mixed economy, it cannot regain a stable and balanced prosperity in industry or commerce. The danger of politically based measures, such as the National Enterprise Board, is that whether they are relevant to the critical situation in which the nation finds itself or not, they tend to be divisive at a time when the nation needs unity of purpose if it is to achieve its objectives. Businessmen who feel themselves beleaguered by politicians are not likely to take the difficult decisions necessary for industrial survival. What the nation needs is the achievement of a more central position from which could be found agreement across all strata of society on what needs to be done to find the way back to real prosperity and balanced growth.

It is necessary to face up to the problem and to find a way of improving contact at the interface between government and industry. All democratically elected governments have a right to implement the proposals on which they have based their appeal to the electorate. But in the past they have not pushed their programme to the point where it is made impossible for businessmen to co-operate, whatever their political views. There must be an area where the national need can prevail and where men of opposing political views can sit down together, as they did in the British National Export Council, to plan co-operation in the national interest. It is, above all, the task of a prime minister to create these conditions on behalf of his government.

Businessmen too have to try to meet politicians halfway. They must not lock themselves in their ivory tower of privilege and sectional interest, but must be willing to meet on neutral ground, if the need is genuine and the government of the day is willing to show itself responsive to it.

A NATIONAL PLAN

The hard pressure of events force the conclusion that what is needed is a national plan for industrial survival to which all parties in the state can give their support. Such a plan is more likely to be well thought out and acceptable if it can be formulated within the framework of machinery that is established and recognised. It must not be a hangover from an election manifesto, or merely a means of winning the co-operation of sections of the population, however powerful they may be. It has to be produced by a joint effort in which management, employees and the state all play their part. In operation it must be based on an involved participative workforce of management and employees, so that its requirements are fully and quickly met and maintained.

Many people today in Britain would doubt the existence of the national will or the appropriate machinery to create this spirit of unity. They could be proved wrong by events, provided the need was made clear. This is not a political treatise, and the pros and cons of what a prime minister can do to unite the nation in a new sense of purpose is not an argument for these pages. What is pertinent to the study of a plan for industrial survival is whether the means are there, if the will is there. Britain's economic circumstances may well deteriorate to the point where, whether the nation likes it or not, there will be an urgent requirement for swift decision. If the means are there to shape such a decision, they may well be the catalyst from which a national will for survival will grow, producing its own leadership in the process.

THE NATIONAL ECONOMIC DEVELOPMENT COUNCIL

In Chapter 6 the present short-comings of the NEDC were discussed. It must be emphasised again that these are the fault, not of NEDO (the National Economic Development Council Office) or NEDC as such, but rather of its tripartite members. Government has not taken its work seriously enough. The Confederation of British Industry and Trades Union Congress have too often regarded Neddy as merely a talking shop. All have shrunk from giving it any kind of real decision-making role. Yet this is what it needs. Successive governments in or out of Parliament, the CBI and the TUC have failed to get the kind of national agreement on national problems that is vital to success. Let us take only the three examples that form the underlying theme of this study. There has been no agreement on: (a) the correct scale of the national effort *vis-à-vis* Britain's world competitors, (b) the right basis for a productive relationship between people at work, or (c) the right long-term relationship between industry and government in a mixed economy. Yet without firm agreement and continuity of purpose in these areas the nation cannot survive as an industrial power of any significance.

This might be what a small left wing minority of the population wants, but it is certainly not what the vast majority requires from those who lead the country inside or outside Parliament.

The main purpose of an enlarged restructured NEDO and NEDC, supported by a sectoral framework of Economic Development Councils, would be to provide the neutral ground where agreement on these and other basic issues would be achieved. In case this is thought to be a theoretical approach, I must quote the requirements for long-term prosperity set out in 'Industry and Government', published by the CBI in the autumn of 1974:

'A renewal of confidence is essential if Industry is to plan for the long term. Lead times for major investment programmes are such that vast sums of capital must be committed well ahead of profitable production. Yet Governments inevitably respond to short term political pressures. One party coming into office seeks to undo whatever in its predecessor's actions does not fit in with its own philosophy.

'Europe is perhaps the best current example of how radical shifts in policy can damage our trading opportunities. Although the present Government does show some signs of having modified its initial hostility to the idea of the EEC as such, CBI has already detected evidence that its earlier intransigence may have had an adverse effect on Britain's export prospects. In addition, a number of established European and other foreign customers seem to have been inhibited by the prospect that their private sector contacts in the UK might be brought under Government control. Overseas customers must have faith in the continuation of the free enterprise system if exports are to continue to grow.

'This is all the more vital at a time when Britain obviously faces an extremely grave economic prospect and one which may get worse before it gets better. We may have to face a long haul before the country is once again on the high road to growth and rising prosperity.

'In this situation it is vital, both for industry and the nation at large, that the basic long term economic objectives adopted for Britain should be clear, should encourage the maximum degree of entrepreneurial skill in a free enterprise society, and should embody the promise of such stability that they will not be disrupted by successive governments.

'CBI believes that discussion through NEDC and the existing consultative machinery is now essential to agree such outline objectives. The Government, the TUC and CBI must all be willing to commit themselves to their attainment, not in the next three to six months but over a span of five to ten years.

'The Government should then concentrate on performing its basic functions efficiently. It should state a minimum body of rules to which society expects all its members, personal and corporate, to conform; and it should encourage market forces—particularly international market forces and competition—to provide the driving force in Industry and hence in the bulk of the economy.

'Free enterprise has shown itself, as a matter of historic record, the best way both of creating wealth and combining economic with political freedom.'

Looked at from a management point of view, the overriding need certainly is for a long period of firm and settled management of the British economy. It is clearly difficult, if not impossible, for the present political set-up, with a fundamentally divided House of Commons, to provide such a lead. As no one has yet invented a better system than the present form of democratic government, this system has to be supplemented by some organisation that can invent and implement a plan for national recovery, founded upon national agreement as the basic principle of the plan. This organisation must not in any way seek to override Parliament, and the first major problem of restructuring the NEDC is how to align it with the existing machinery of democratic government.

INDUSTRY AND PARLIAMENT

Industry is, on the whole, not well represented in Parliament, yet the majority of parliamentary decisions today have industrial implications. Earlier in this study it has been shown that political and industrial decision making are often incompatible because the requirements of Parliament and of industry are quite different. When the existing parliamentary machinery is examined in search of neutral ground, it is impossible not to notice the marked difference of approach to industry to be found in debate in the Commons and the Lords as compared with discussion in parliamentary select committees. The Committee on Expenditure and the Parliamentary Scientific Committee, for example, are in many cases more searching in their inquiries than the House of Commons, but they operate from much more practical baselines. It would in no way interfere with normal parliamentary practice if Parliament were to establish a 'Trade and Industry Select Committee'. This, following precedent, would represent all parties in the House with a majority for the government party. It would elect its own Chairman and would have the right, as have other select committees, to send for people and papers; senior civil servants, industrialists and trade unionists could all give evidence. Among the papers to be studied would be a number arising from the proceedings of the NEDC. Such a committee could conveniently provide the parliamentary link between the NEDC and the back benches, in the same way as ministers and civil servants provide the link between the NEDC and Parliament as a whole. The proceedings of the select committee would be presented to Parliament and thus would be debated. NEDC proceedings would be presented at least in summary form to the select committee, which would have the right to examine the Director General of the NEDC on the council's work. There would thus be an element of parliamentary control of the NEDC, to supplement the governmental control exercised through the chairmanship of the council by the Chancellor of the Exchequer or some other senior minister.

Ultimate responsibility for a national plan must be taken by the government and supported by Parliament. But the plan would be constructed on the basis of NEDC debate and recommendation. Its performance monitoring would also fall to the NEDC and EDCs. Parliament would have its normal opportunities of debating and questioning the national plan as presented by government. It would also have the double check of the report of its own parliamentary select committee on the detailed proposals and working of the plan. In consideration of full parliamentary accountability in this way, there would have to be agreement between the government and opposition that the basic framework of the plan would not be destroyed by a change of government. There might be an advantage here in providing some opposition membership of the NEDC as a further guarantee of continuity. It cannot be emphasised too strongly that managers cannot do their job efficiently without some guarantee that there will not be change for change's sake in the conditions within which they have to operate. Politicians of all parties must take more account of the facts of industrial growth and development. These industrial realities require time cycles far longer than the period normally provided by a single government. If the practice of trying to stand the economy on its head every four or five years is continued, then there can be no hope of successful and consistent planning by management for industrial and economic recovery.

THE NEDC AND OTHER GOVERNMENT AGENCIES

It is necessary, therefore, to examine the NEDC in relation both to other government agencies and to the machinery of government itself. It must be accepted that the NEDC cannot in any way supersede Parliament, but unless it can be enabled to play a more decisive role in the machinery of government it is doomed to remain largely ineffective. Here the proposal put forward in the 1974 TUC review of policy seems attractive; namely, the suggestion that the NEDC should have the right to 'overview' the work of the other government agencies.

On the assumption, which must be made, that government policy can only move forwards again in the context of a national plan, the mechanics of the plan could be something like the following. Discussions in the NEDC, based on policy initiatives from the CBI, the TUC and independent members, would identify the problems and indicate at least the broad outlines of the solutions. These proposals would draw on the work done in the EDCs and trade associations, which would have the task of highlighting company and sectoral problems and solutions.

The government would give its initial reactions to these proposals in the NEDC and would contribute its own ideas. It would have to accept that this situation would give rise to debate in NEDC. The government would have to modify its own proposals, as would the other parties to the discussion to get broad agreement strategy.

Then the government would of course take over and, through its own machinery, bring final proposals to the Cabinet and present them to Parliament as a White Paper or, if further national discussion were required, in NEDC and elsewhere as a Green Paper. Finally Parliament would decide on the appropriate measures. It is at this point that most past failures have occurred. Parliament and governments are good at initiating policy, but singularly bad at monitoring its progress towards success. Here the NEDC would have a distinctive part to play in monitoring progress at both national and sectoral level through the EDCs and trade associations.

Departments of state would make their appropriate contribution to all these processes, but the NEDC would represent the industrial last word to government. Obviously the council would have no part to play in party political discussions without industrial implications. As an example of relationships between departmental agencies and the NEDC, the National Enterprise Board might be taken. Some of its exponents have seen a supranational role for this body but, in fact, organisations such as this should have a useful supporting and co-ordinating role, but no more. The National Enterprise Board and planning agreements could well supplement the general work of the NEDC and EDCs. The board could look after the state interest in government-owned companies or where government had a substantial shareholding. It could be the focus for government help to individual concerns where the overall liability, such as in the case of British Leyland, was too large to be handled by City institutions alone. It could also, in collaboration with the appropriate EDC, aid in an efficiency audit of an industry or sector. It might well look at the structure of some of the nationalised industries. Always the NEDC would have the 'overview' of the total national plan and its implementation.

THE NEDC AND THE GRASS ROOTS

Now comes the crux of the problem, as far as the successful implementation of a national plan is concerned. Previous failures have arisen because of a lack of conviction and collaboration at sectoral and finally at shopfloor levels. Politicians, and perhaps others at the top of the national structure, too easily forget that words, whether enshrined in Act of Parliament or departmental edict, mean nothing unless they are implemented by people. This is still so even where politicians have to invoke the law as their instrument of implementation. No national plan has any hope of long-term success unless it is based on willing and co-operative implementation at shopfloor and social grass roots level. The chance of acceptance in this way, by the broad mass of the population, would be greatly enhanced if the plan were built from the bottom up, and this could best be achieved by NEDC recommendations arising from sectoral and local needs, through the machinery of the EDCs and the trade associations working closely with them. Success here would also presuppose that participation in the processes of decision making at company level had been widely and successfully achieved. On this basis the non-governmental members of the NEDC would be unlikely to advocate policies which they knew could not be made to 'stick' at company or trade union branch level. It would be their task, in the implementation phase, to be responsible for the monitoring and therefore the carrying-out of policy at this level. They would, therefore, have to be sure that they were correctly interpreting the views of the EDCs, trade associations and union branches in the policies that they put forward.

This process implies a much higher degree of participation in all sectors of British industrial life, but to exchange time lost in disputes procedure for time spent in policy discussion would seem to be no bad thing. It is a new concept for management and trade unions alike and it implies a much wider degree of knowledge of one another's business, but revolutions are not implemented by a refusal to change procedures. It would be no less than a beneficial revolution if Britain found a way of harnessing its total industrial power to the task of creating a new era of balanced growth and prosperity. A claim such as this must be tested, so far as it is possible, against known facts. Let us take as an example the problem that has most plagued the British economy in these postwar years, namely, the problem of wages and prices.

All British governments since the war have sought to achieve full employment, a rising standard of living and a stable balance of payments. There have been many variations on the theme, but on the whole the first two aims have been achieved at some sacrifice of the third. Now circumstances have been fundamentally changed. The relatively fragile British economy has not been able to stand the shock of the sudden transition from world expansion to recession which has been triggered by the quadrupling of the price of oil. In the free-for-all that has followed the increase, the exercise of industrial muscle in Britain has, for the first time in the postwar period, created a situation where the government of the day can successfully implement none of the above three policies. Unemployment, the cost of living and the balance of payments were all running beyond any reasonable control in the first half of 1975.

Yet much of this imbalance could have been corrected if the relationship between wages and prices could have been discussed on the neutral ground of the NEDC. Here the facts of a Britain living on borrowed money, and therefore borrowed industrial time, could have been made plain. These national facts could have been related to sectoral and company needs on the basis of proposals emanating from local level. On this basis a wage contract might have been achieved that would have been related to reality—one that had the support and understanding of all in industry. It is interesting to note that when the government in July 1975 was forced by events to act against inflation and took up the six pounds a week initiative proposed by Jack Jones, it immediately found that it had to make greater use of NEDC and the tripartite approach to help make the bargain stick.

AN NEDC WAGES–PRICES CONTRACT

As the government accepted at the time, the emergency anti-inflation measures of July 1975 (The Attack on Inflation) have to be followed by a long-term plan. Such a plan must obviously concern itself with wages as well as other matters. A real wages contract must be built on discussion and disclosure of the facts at shopfloor level. These facts would cover, for example, the cost of re-equipment and capital investment at current replacement values, the difficulties of cash flow at a 20 per cent rate of inflation and the falling percentage of profit in real terms. Facts such as these would in no way conflict with the normal processes of collective bargaining, but as they came up to the NEDC through the trade associations and EDCs they would provide a practical basis for discussion. This would enable the

NEDC to discuss the possibility of a national earnings contract rather than a contract concerned solely with basic wage rates. Let us take the Engineering Employers' Federation for an example: basic rates very rarely bear much relevance to 'take-home pay', yet it is take-home pay related to prices that is the real value equation for the employee, and for the manager for that matter. Through the NEDC there would be much scope for discussion of productivity and earnings related to output in manufacturing industry and to efficiency in service industry and the public service. The government would have to make its contribution in terms of encouragement to capital investment or of changes in earned-income tax rules.

Obviously these points touch only the fringe of the multitudinous problems that affect the take-home pay–prices equation. Yet if these were discussed against a background of knowledge and agreement, at shopfloor and sectoral level, the nation might be in sight of the kind of wages and salary contract that would stimulate output and efficiency without increasing costs and prices. Earnings justified by increased output and efficiency are not inflationary. Earnings underpinned in this way should be the goal of the two triangles of industrial power. The company triangle would be built on the base of plant consultation and participation and would reach its apex in discussions at board level between directors and employees. The national triangle would be built on the base of sectoral consultation and participation through the trade associations and EDCs and would reach its apex in the NEDC. Only in this way can an end be made to the ritual dance of negotiations about unreal issues, which leads to those with most industrial power being paid 'Dane geld' without any reference to the longer-term national interest.

A NEW APPROACH TO NATIONAL PLANNING

With the NEDC expanded and used in this way the nation could move forward to a new approach to national planning.

This would be, not a stereotyped plan produced in isolation in Whitehall and stuck with an unrealisable growth target, but rather a plan for a nationwide structure built with industry's own policy bricks. Such a plan would in no way remove from the Treasury and the Department of State their proper contribution to such a plan. In the end it must be a 'government' plan, built up within the machinery of government. Its chances of acceptance would be enormously enhanced if the proposals had the practical backing of the NEDC following the discussion procedures outlined above. Its chances of success in operation would similarly be enhanced by practical monitoring through the NEDC and EDCs down to shopfloor level. In this way Britain could correct the mistakes that have been made over the postwar period through failure to achieve a satisfactory understanding between industry and government. Coupled with the plan outlined in Chapter 7 for participation at shopfloor level, this could lead to a new approach to economic and industrial planning at all levels in government, industry and the trade unions. From this could spring a new incentive for managers to create a stronger and more efficient nation, where each contributor to the national product knew what he had to do and did it in the knowledge that the more he earned the better it was for him and for the nation as a whole.

THE PROBLEM OF PROPORTION

Finally, there is the third basic national requirement of proportion and scale. Britain's best opportunity today is to be an efficient productive member of the European Economic Community of nations; alone the country would have little or no chance of industrial or any other kind of prosperity. So continued membership of the EEC provides the measure by which the scale of future British commitments can be judged. Advanced projects on the frontiers of technology, such as Concorde, must clearly be planned on a European basis. A European basis would also offer considerable savings in defence costs, if a real European family of weapons could be developed. Here, and in many other ways (nuclear research, for example), Britain's advanced technology can make a contribution that is within the acceptable limits of national costs and resources.

It is not only advanced technology projects that need reconsideration if Britain is to have a well-balanced industrial base. Study must be made of the growing imbalance between productive and non-productive workers and managers. For example, the growth of local and national government service, and its demands on manpower, represent a transference from those who contribute to righting Britain's balance of payments to those who increase its national overheads and thus the burden on the balance of payments. Here again, problems such as this need the discipline of discussion on a practical basis and on neutral party political grounds. The whole problem of the size and scale of the national effort would be an essential background to any NEDC proposals for a national plan for balanced growth.

RELATIONS WITH EUROPE AND THE INDUSTRIAL
WORLD

If there were no other fundamental reason for Britain to put her industrial house in order by proper management, adequate motive would be provided by the country's need to earn its living in a highly competitive world. Britain's national resources show that it will never be as self-sufficient in food and many raw materials as are a lot of its industrial competitors. Nor should the country look forward optimistically to North Sea oil as the main factor that will create future prosperity, as it may be deceiving itself. The cost of a barrel of North Sea oil will be so high, even on the basis of inflation to date, that it will offer Arab producers every chance of holding their prices at a level that could make British oil an uneconomic source of energy.

There is, in fact, no easy way out for Britain, no soft option.

In the end the British will have to pay their own way in the world, or to cut back on their standard of living and abandon any hope of maintaining anything like full employment. Whatever the politicians of all parties may wish to do, their policies will have to conform to these harsh facts.

Chapter 9

THE NEW APPROACH

The purpose of this study of industry over the postwar period has been to endeavour to show that, if certain lessons could be learned and applied, Britain could look forward to a period of renewed and balanced growth and development. Such a desirable state of affairs will not transpire unless all those involved are willing to make a new approach to both their own problems and those of the nation as a whole. The British can destroy themselves and the only remedial force that can avoid the tragedy is, again, themselves. There is no easy solution to be promoted by some demagogic messiah, that will avoid the painful tasks ahead. So, once again, a study has to be made of the hard and factual possibilities, to see what elements could form the basis of a new approach to the challenge of industrial survival for Britain.

The three main themes of this present study do not pretend to be all-embracing, but they could form the basis for a new approach to the nation's problems. If the scale of attack can be got right, if the full ability and vigour of the British people are harnessed, if a new and more fruitful working partnership between industry and government can be achieved, then surely the way to recovery must lie ahead. The achievement of these goals requires the backing and understanding of all managers and employees; it also requires certain specific actions on the part of government, employers and employees. The correct point of decision making for the government, the Confederation of British Industry, representing employers, and the Trades Union Congress, representing employees, is the National Economic Development Council, but this organi-

sation cannot play a more decisive role unless its constituent
bodies are willing to rethink their own philosophy.

THE GOVERNMENT

A new approach for government, *any* government, except one
that rejects the concept of a mixed economy entirely, must be
based on the necessity of harnessing the total potential of
industrial and commercial Britain. It is difficult to see how
this can be achieved except from the middle ground of politics.
Some would draw a conclusion from this that what is needed
is some form of national government. Events may well neces-
sitate such a development, but it will be a short-lived and
uneasy administration, like any other possible government,
until there is a greater acceptance of the real facts of the
position in which the nation now finds itself.

Britain's present heavy and increasing foreign indebtedness
may still be capable of being contained within the compass of
the new funds generated by North Sea oil, but soon the future
of this country's one new source of national income will have
been totally mortgaged. This will still be so, although in a
larger timescale, even if the present balance-of-payments
crisis is got under control. So the British have no justifications
for paying themselves more than they earn or for running the
economy on borrowed money. If this criterion is strictly applied,
as it must be, it will bring about a sharp fall in the standard of
living and a further rise in unemployment unless the country's
current assets can be better deployed. The chief of these is the
skill of British men and women applied to (a) creating and
manufacturing goods for export, (b) managing Britain's
overseas trade, (c) creating invisible exports through financial
expertise in the City of London, and (d) producing more
food and energy at home to lessen the country's overall export
bill. It is an asset almost wholly dependent on the successful
operation of the free enterprise sector of the economy. Only
individuals, organisations and companies organised and

managed on the basis of free enterprise provide what is in truth the financial foundation of the state. It is free enterprise that is providing the exports, the employment and the tax revenues essential for the well-being of the British.

In these circumstances there seems to be no possible justification for seeking to further increase state interference in free enterprise areas. Government should rather concentrate on creating a favourable climate for free enterprise, providing the maximum incentive by encouraging the market economy and free competition. In the state-owned sector and the nationalised industries it should concentrate on achieving a much higher level of efficiency and productivity. In the particular case of nationalised industry, it should encourage chairmen and their boards to run their undertakings on the principles of free enterprise and should divorce them as far as possible from direct government control. It would be implicit in this whole policy that the present 'mix' of the economy would not be further disturbed, one way or the other. There would also be an intention by all political parties to avoid contentious and divisive legislation and to contain government within the bounds of financial and social administration as far as possible. Where new legislative developments were involved, with industrial or commercial implications, these would only be proceeded with after full discussion in the NEDC and, as far as possible, by the general support of the three parties involved in the council.

This admittedly modest and low key approach by government would require the avoidance of excess elsewhere and employers and employees would have to follow suit. In these areas it would be for government, not to impose new controls, but rather to operate those that exist in a more effective manner. There would have to be continuing attempts to iron out extremes of wealth or poverty, but these are achievable within the present tax arrangements. There would also have to be a more orderly arrangement for collective bargaining, especially in state-owned and nationalised industry. Rewards should be related to unit costs in productive industries and to operating efficiency in service industries. There would be a fruitful field of discussion here for the NEDC, which should lead the attempt to replace the present structure of wage bargaining by earnings linked to productivity and efficiency. Again, no further legislation is required, nor is the use of wage or price controls by legislative means. The 1975 crisis over wages and prices shows how vital it is to find a new basis for the control of these factors in any plan to defeat inflation.

With some of the present legislative overburden taken off Whitehall and Parliament, more attention could be given to sound and practical administration, as far as the Civil Service was concerned, and to the control of expenditure, as far as Parliament was concerned. 'Supply days', when Parliament now approves financial estimates formally and the opposition takes the time for a debate of its own choosing, could actually become supply days, when the supply of finance to the government was examined and criticised in detail. Parliament should also have more time for the work of its own select committees and particularly for the proposed new 'trade and industry' committee. This committee would be, not an appendage of the present Expenditure Committee, but rather a sovereign body of equal stature with its own staff. If parliamentary time at Westminister were somewhat reduced, few Members of Parliament would complain. Most would gain, as would their constituents, from closer and more regular contacts at constituency level. It would, of course, be totally unrealistic to pretend that such a concept of the work of Government and Parliament is in line with the views of sections of the militant left of the socialist party or of the Communist Party.

There is a small section of the Labour Party and the trade unions which desires to destroy free enterprise as it exists at present. What they would put in its place remains ill-defined, but their present thinking seems to indicate a form of state control of a rather less efficient model than that practised in the USSR. The 1975 referendum issue served to highlight the true position of the left wing in its desire to break with Europe.

Remaining in Europe will not necessarily curb its long-term desires, but their overwhelming defeat in the referendum does provide a breathing space for those who believe in the efficiently managed free enterprise system and the maintenance of the present 'mix' in the economy. Both systems, however, require management, and there may be a few managers who prefer the rigidity of the state-controlled system. They would be well advised to examine what the continued expansion of such a system would do to Britain's parliamentary democracy and industrial prosperity. The majority of managers support the concept that the parliamentary mix itself is now constituted in a way that favours state control and limits free enterprise to an undesirable degree.

Economic freedom and democratic freedom must go hand in hand. Economic and industrial dictatorship by the state will always be the enemy of political liberty. Such a system rejects freedom of choice in favour of 'Whitehall knows best'. Destroy freedom of economic choice and, in the end, freedom of democratic choice will be destroyed as well. The converse is equally true: a well-managed system of free enterprise makes freedom of choice its main discipline, and freedom of choice for the customer and for the voter go together. The manager who believes in the profession of management as being the exercise of choice and decision making in a free society will have to take more account of his duty as an elector, if he wants to retain his present way of life and a chance to improve it. As the report on 'Industry and Government' said, 'A market economy is the economic aspect of political democracy.' Very careful heed should be taken of moves to elevate state intervention into being a political as well as an industrial way of life for all in Britain.

THE CONFEDERATION OF BRITISH INDUSTRY

Government, then, should pull back to a more classical stance, holding the ring by concerning itself with defence, law and order and sound financial administration. The reverse policy is desirable for the CBI, which must become a more activist body, seeking to change the course of events rather than just reacting to them. Yet its constitution is not entirely suited to such a role. The CBI, like Topsy, 'just growed' out of the old Federation of British Industry and the British Employers' Confederation. Its decision-making body, the 'Grand Council', is some 400 strong and comprises representatives of powerful trade associations, such as the Engineering Employers' Federation, as well as individual members. Although it has representation from banking, the City and the retail trade, it primarily revolves at present around the pivot of the 100 top manufacturing companies. In government eyes it is a convenient representative of industry and often tends to be asked to speak for a wider constituency than its members in fact fully represent. In the public gaze it is a kind of opposite number to the TUC and thus is subject to the opprobrium that rests on all trade unions whether they represent the bosses or the workers.

In fact, it is surprising and greatly to the credit of successive presidents and directors general that the CBI actually represents anything. Its structure of a Grand Council and a large network of internal and often overlapping policy committees is not well suited to the making of long-term policy or to instant reaction to events. The council meets only monthly, its committees are largely advisory to the council and the confederation, by its very structure, represents many diverse interests including the nationalised industries. If the CBI is to play a significant role in shaping national policy—either through the NEDC, directly to the Prime Minister and senior members of his Cabinet or by influencing public opinion—then its structure has to change. So do its relationships with the British Institute of Management, the Institute of Directors and other bodies such as the chambers of commerce and the Retail Consortium.

The CBI has to face a changed industrial world. Government intervention in major industry continues; Rolls-Royce, Ferranti and British Leyland are only three of the recent examples. The area of nationalised industry threatens eventually to include

aerospace and shipbuilding. Every company can face direct
intervention in its affairs through devices such as the National
Enterprise Board or planning agreements. So the old CBI
tradition of 'representing' the views of its members to government and reacting to events is no longer appropriate. In a
world where militancy and industrial muscle count, the CBI
too has to become militant and activist when it suits the
interests of its members.

**The need is for two strong organisations within the
CBI: one comprising the professional paid staff heading
up to the Director General; the other being the voluntary
office bearers heading up to the President, who himself
will have to give the CBI most of his attention during
his years of office.** Both organisations must spread the load
of meetings, speeches and representations of various kinds.
The structure best suited to this would be to change the CBI's
committee structure to match the government's own machine.
Each senior minister should have his CBI shadow, in a manner
somewhat similar to the practice followed by the opposition in
Parliament. The President should also have his own 'shadow
cabinet' and the recent device of a President's 'advisory panel'
opens the way for this.

The CBI would not have the same cabinet structure as
government. The Grand Council must retain the final power
of approving policy, but the President's panel would play an
important advisory role and co-ordinate the work of the chairmen of the leading CBI committees including the Smaller
Firms Committee and the Regional Organisation of the
Confederation. The Director General could have a similar
in-house cabinet. In this way each department of state in
government would be faced by a senior businessman as
chairman of the appropriate CBI committee, each supported
by an appropriate full-time CBI official of 'director' status as
his permanent secretary and backed by an administrative
team. Having achieved this structure, which in part already
exists, the President and the Director General should encourage

each of their 'ministers', the committee chairmen, to speak and promote the work of his committee as a minister does for his department.

So much for day-to-day policy. Beyond this the CBI must try more successfully to influence the general public and the electorate as a way of supporting the longer-term policy objectives which it will be promoting in the NEDC and directly with government. The first broadly based experiment of this kind was the work of a small but high level CBI steering committee which I was asked to chair in the second half of 1974. This committee produced, in a fairly short time, 'Industry and Government', a statement of national policy. Two popular editions—one in wall chart form, the other entitled 'Let Industry Work'—were produced and discussed with Members of Parliament of all parties, editors and principals of universities and business schools. Had the committee been earlier off the mark it might have made a greater impression on the October election. As it was, its work was overtaken by the actual election campaign. However, it was a useful prototype exercise and showed that the CBI could co-ordinate the views of its internal committees, transmute them into a coherent policy unanimously supported by the Grand Council and launch them on the general world of public opinion. The whole operation got a good press and its objective was well summed up in the conclusion of 'Let Industry Work':

> 'Industry then says "hands off" to plans for even more state ownership and control. It believes it would be disastrous to undermine the free enterprise system that creates jobs and rewards for all of us. Co-operation not coercion is the right way to provide the continuity, stability and incentives by which industry can go on increasing the nation's income and wealth and improve its quality of life.'

This was a useful pilot scheme and one that may well have considerable influence on the future structure of the CBI.

As the CBI clears its own mind it must seek to work more fruitfully with other bodies. The CBI is about nothing if it is not about the efficient management of a free enterprise society, so its relationships with the British Institute of Management have always been close. The institute is by its charter a non-political body and contains civil servants and trade unionists on its Council. It cannot therefore take the more politically activist role of the CBI of the future, but it can collaborate much more closely in seeing that the management voice is heard in policy making and that managers as they increase in seniority can bridge the gap between membership and chairmanship of the Council and committees of the British Institute of Management, and membership of the CBI's Grand Council and membership and chairmanship of its committees. The Chairman of the Institute's Council is, of course, an *ex officio* member of the Confederation's Grand Council. The British Institute of Management too must spread its net more widely and seek to link together all the professional associations that have an interest in management. The experience of Sir Frederick Catherwood, as Chairman of its Council, has provided an excellent working base for this expansion. Relations with the chambers of commerce have already been greatly improved by Sir Ralph Bateman in his term as President of the CBI, who in this way has added another useful chapter to the important unifying work for which he will be remembered in the CBI.

The Institute of Directors, however, is a more difficult problem. Founded by General Sir Louis Spears as very much a right wing 'bosses' trade union', its development owes a very great deal to its first Director General, Sir Richard Powell. Under his leadership it has acquired over 40,000 members, all individual directors, and a strong representation overseas in the Commonwealth. Its annual showpiece, the Albert Hall conference, has always succeeded in attracting leading world figures to take part. Yet somehow, perhaps because of its 'plushy' headquarters in Belgrave Square and its concern among other things with directors' artistic consciousnesses and health, it has remained what its original founders intended—a lively well-organised institute from which directors, as individuals, can derive much benefit but which finds it difficult to adopt a more representative role. Yet it too has a deep interest in free enterprise and its survival. In the battle which free enterprise must fight and win to survive, this Institute could have a vital part to play.

So times must change for the CBI and its allies. They must find a new impetus and new means of impressing both the public and Parliament with the need to defend the British free way of life, which is so intrinsically associated with free enterprise and freedom of choice. The policy link between the CBI and the chambers of commerce is an indication of how this could be achieved.

THE TRADES UNION CONGRESS

It is unrealistic to discuss the contribution that the trade unions could make to a new approach to national problems without taking account of the changes that have taken place in their structure in the postwar period. In the late 1940s and early 1950s, as I know from my own experience, the more powerful unions were commanded by leaders of a calibre similar to Ernest Bevin's. Bill Carron of the Amalgamated Union of Engineering Workers, Arthur Deakin of the Transport and General Workers' Union, Tom Williamson of the Municipal and General Workers' Union and Harry Douglas of the Steelworkers' Union were only a few of these. Such men were in firm control of their unions and could deliver a negotiated bargain on the basis of their own surety and judgement. The TUC General Council was therefore a body of significance with some hold over its members. Today power has been diffused and thus dominant leadership at the top has been made much more difficult. So it is not surprising that the militants now make most of the running. The media, particularly television, have aided and abetted this development; confrontation and militancy are news and 'good television', whereas co-operation is not.

It is of great importance for the trade union movement and for the nation as a whole that the authority of the TUC General Council and of the leaders of the movement as a whole be re-established. Governments should have sought to support this end but, probably inadvertently, they have done exactly the reverse. The failure of the Labour government's 'in place of strife' initiative and the even more disastrous failure of the Conservative government's Industrial Relations Act 1971 gave militancy in the trade unions its most powerful boost since pre-war days. Confrontation with a Conservative government also accentuated the polarisation of the trade union movement and involved it even more deeply with only one political party in the nation. More difficult economic times and the inevitable strains on the movement, torn between its duty to its members and its duty to its chosen political party, have now somewhat dimmed the first flush of enthusiasm for the 'We are the masters now' concept. So perhaps the time is coming when the trade union movement may be willing to think again objectively about its position in long-term national affairs. If it decides that its preferred leverage is through even closer association with the Labour Party, then it will condemn itself to a continuing sterile political argument about the place of socialism in political and industrial life. It will also provide endless opportunities for left wing militancy to exploit the situation.

No one could expect with any realism that the TUC, as at present constituted, could break with the Labour Party. But it would clearly be in its interest and that of its members to move to a more central bargaining position in affairs of state. Two factors could prepare the way for a British trade union movement with more power and influence in the state: (a) the recovery of leadership and authority by the TUC General Council; and (b) the adoption of a more central negotiating position, particularly with regard to employers and political parties.

Many people today feel that the trade unions are already too powerful. This is true as far as the exercise of crude industrial muscle power is concerned. But demands from any pressure group backed by threats create their own backlash, and in the final analysis the movement has not got its hands on the ultimate levers of power. The TUC cannot give orders to even a Labour Party Cabinet and it does not control the sources of capital and thus of employment for its members. No party rules for ever, so a trade union movement tied to the Labour Party, and to its left wing at that, is not in a strong long-term bargaining position in a democratic state. Thus the movement's new approach should be to rethink its philosophy and to reshape it to fit the form of economic management that the movement itself advocates; namely, national planning through the central agency of the NEDC and local and sectoral planning through the EDCs. The TUC's view that the NEDC should 'overview' all other government agencies is a sound one. If the TUC is to play its full part with the CBI in making this new concept work, then it will not be able at the same time to involve itself as a corporate body too deeply in the internal politics of socialism. What its individual members do is of course their own responsibility.

Authority and a central negotiating position are what the trade union movement needs if it is to secure long-term influence in national affairs. It can, no doubt, achieve further short-term goals by militancy and pressure exerted on the Labour Party through its own left wing. However, the end of that road is the collectivist state and, as the referendum on the European Economic Community showed, there is no majority for that kind of solution in British democracy at this time. How the General Council may regain its authority is a domestic matter for the trade union movement, but a more democratic base for the election of union officers may help. As far as a more central position in the state is concerned, there are much goodwill and willingness to help in this available from employers at the CBI, providing that a 'British solution' can be found. If the attempt to force companies to adopt totally unsuitable West German or Dutch practices is dropped, much more progress can now be made towards 'participative' management in British industry. The debate as to how this is to be done is essentially a matter for industry, not for Whitehall. It should not be impossible for agreed guidelines to be laid down by the CBI and TUC which would cover new rights for employees and their wider representation on boards of directors. One must hope that the inquiry set up by Peter Shore will take very careful account of this point despite its restrictive terms of reference.

The CBI and TUC are publicly on record as thinking the same about an expanded future for the NEDC. Here is an important field for collaboration where much is already agreed. Real power for the TUC and CBI would lie in an alliance that led to both organisations representing agreed solutions to national problems to the government of the day. No government could refuse to give very careful consideration to such proposals.

THE PEOPLE DECIDE

There is nothing fundamentally wrong with the British people. They would react to a Dunkirk situation today in the same way as they faced an enemy on the French shore in 1940. Economic and political Dunkirks, however, coupled with demagogic leadership, do not produce the shock reaction of overt military defeat. Yet the overwhelming referendum majority in favour of Europe proved that the Britain of today will not reject its obligations once it sees them plainly.

But Britain has no patent for survival. It has lost an empire and could well decline to destruction like past empires and their heartlands have so often done. Britain in Europe provides a way out of this dilemma, but only if the British people react to Europe in a positive and vigorous way. It is said that Parliament works on the basis of the opposition having its say but the government in the end having its way. In a more questioning age this might be rewritten in the form of politicians and activists having their say but in the end the British people having their way. Today the grass roots leaders of the people are those who manage actual situations in business, the professions, the trade unions and government and across the whole of Britain's mixed economy. It is the 'managers' who can implement the blueprint for Britain's survival and recovery. Given an understanding of the true facts they will do just that.